This book belongs to:

____

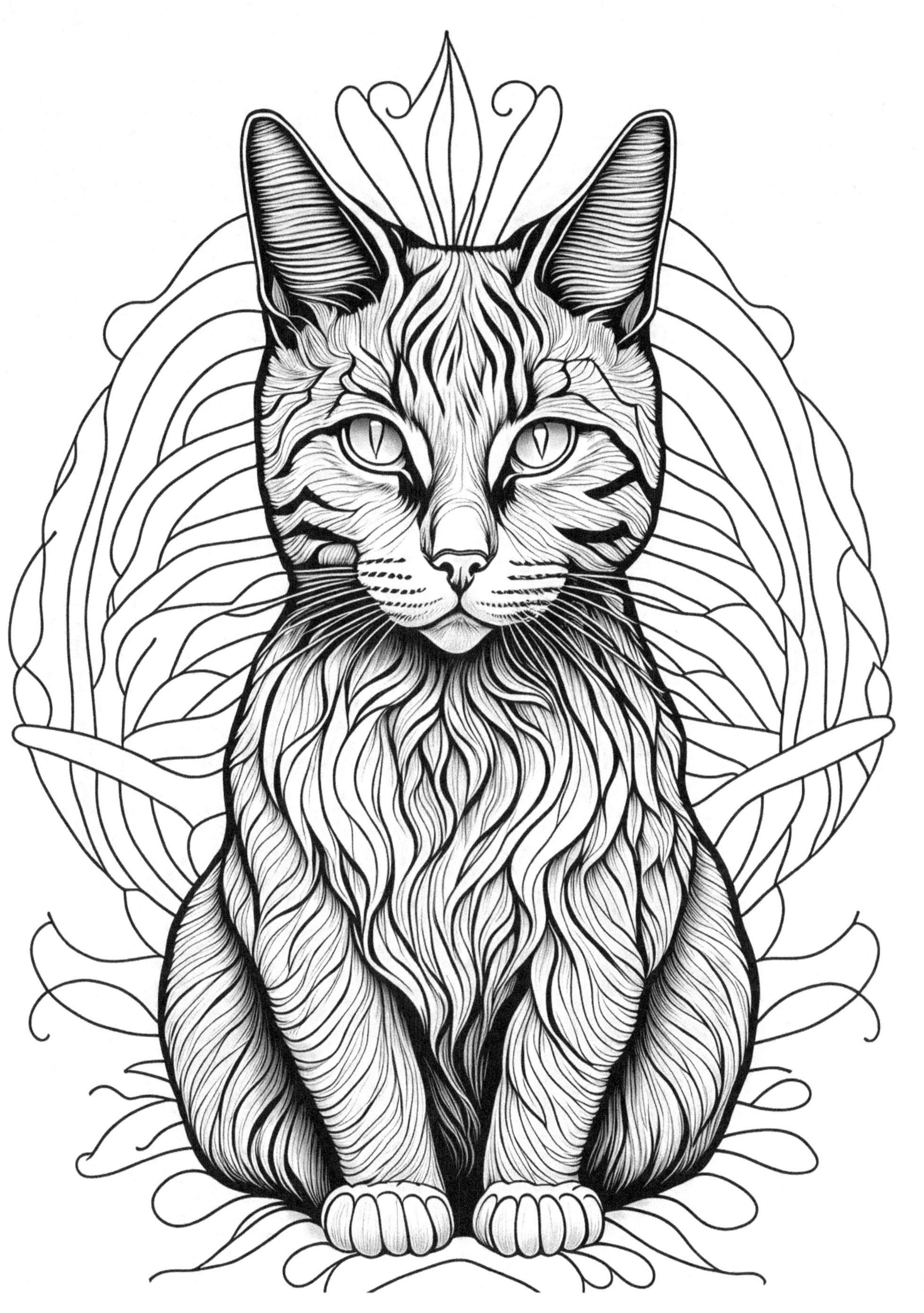

American bobtail cat

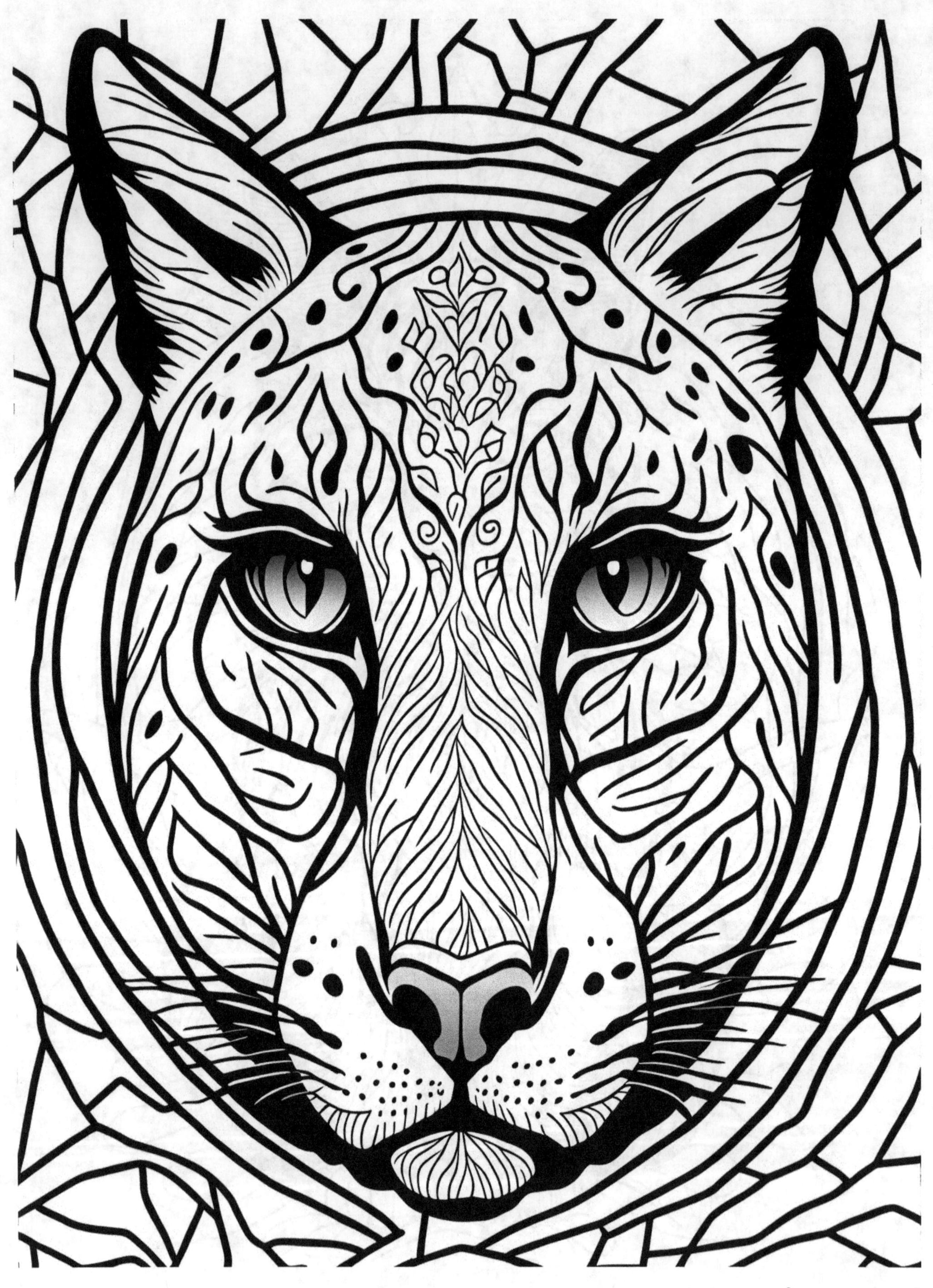

Amur leopard

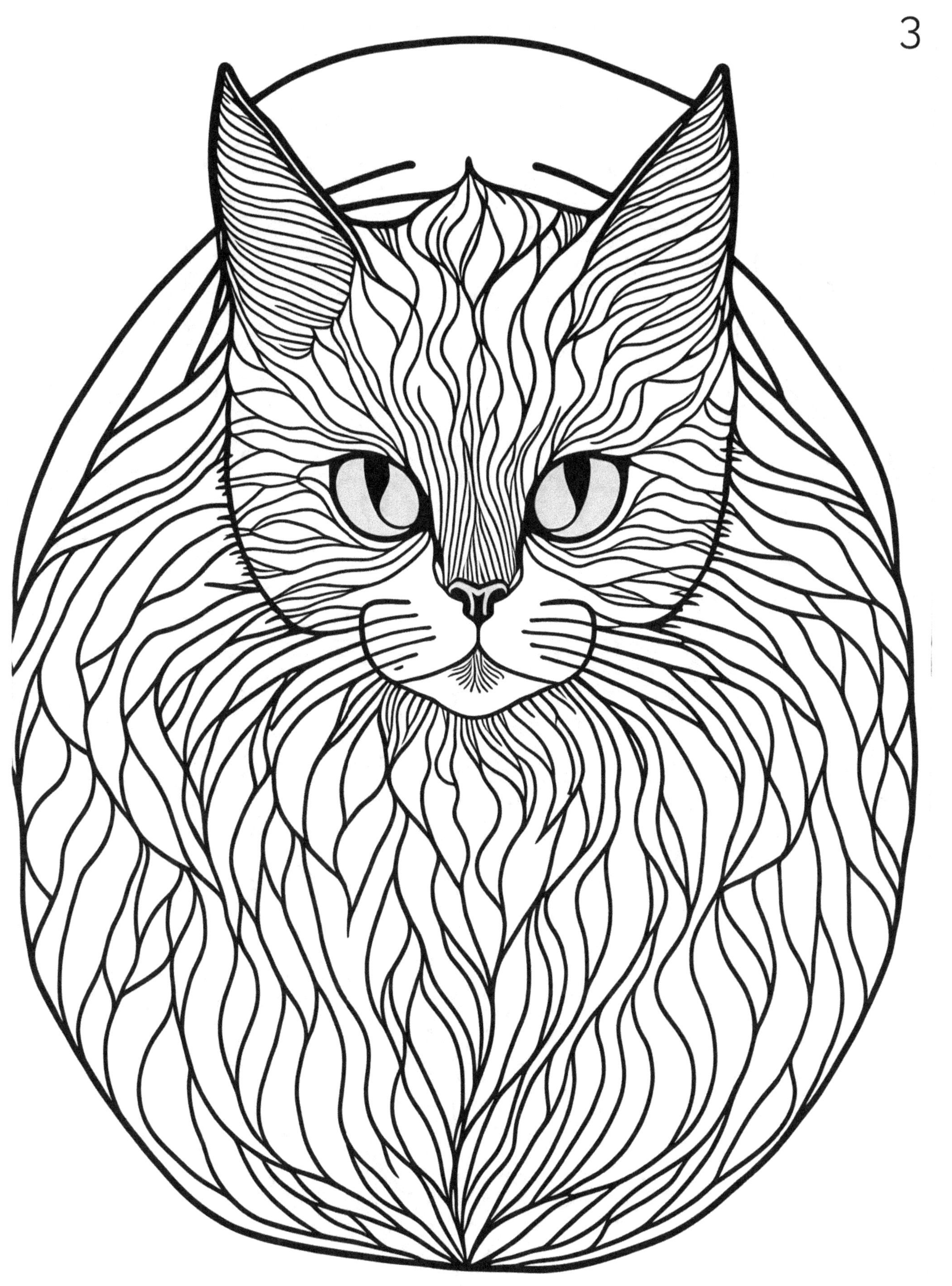

Angora bobtail cat

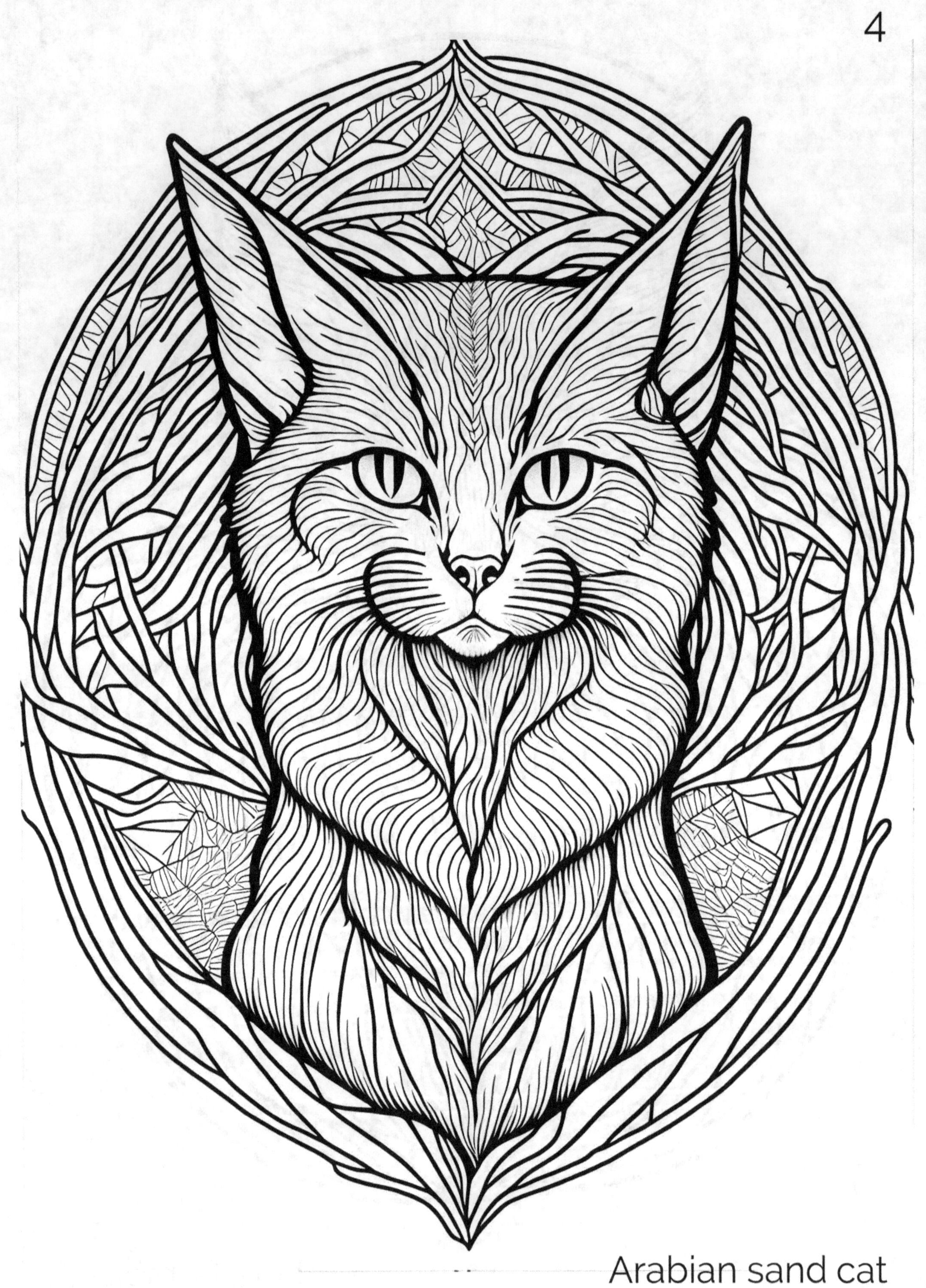

Arabian sand cat

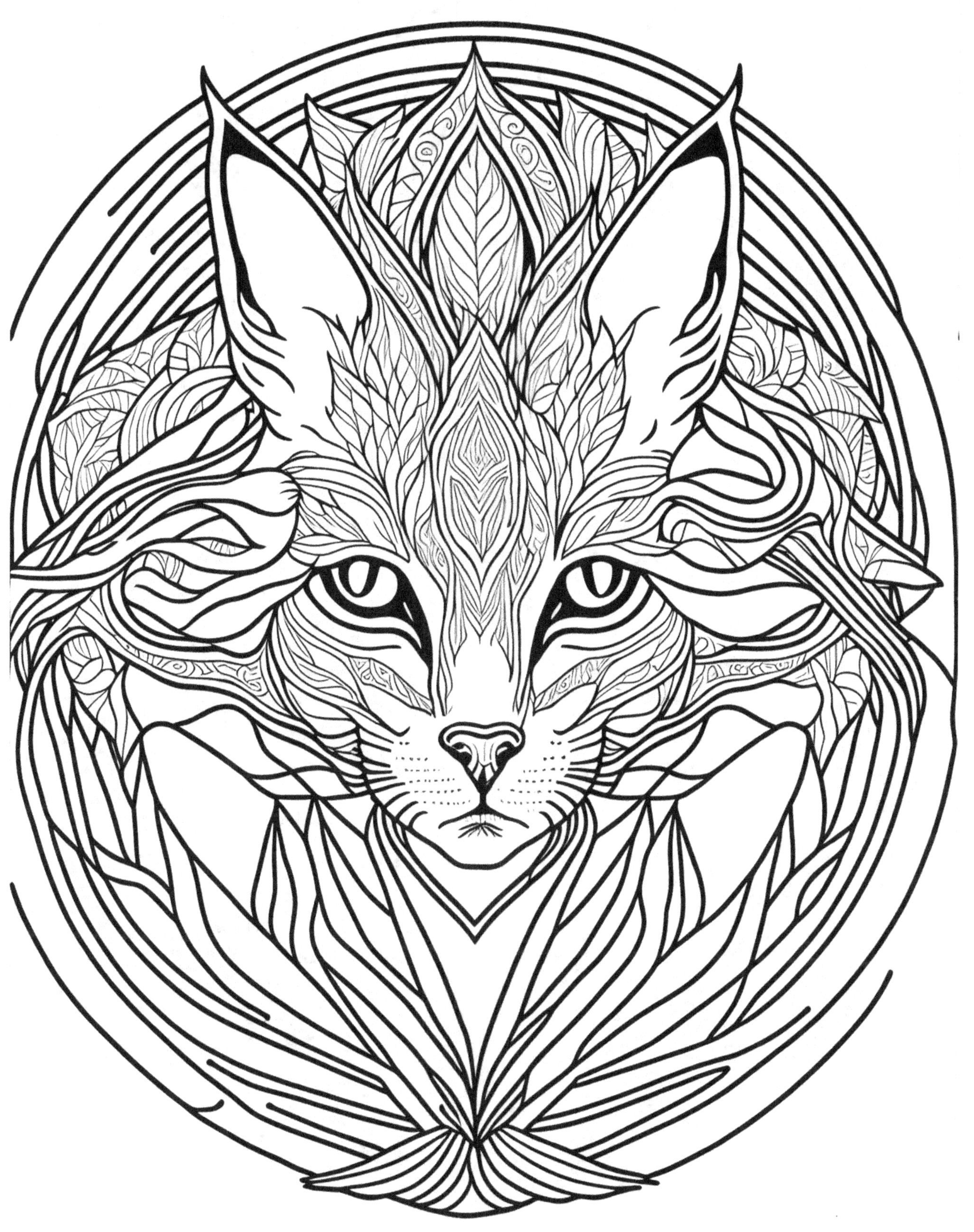

Arabian sand dune desert cat

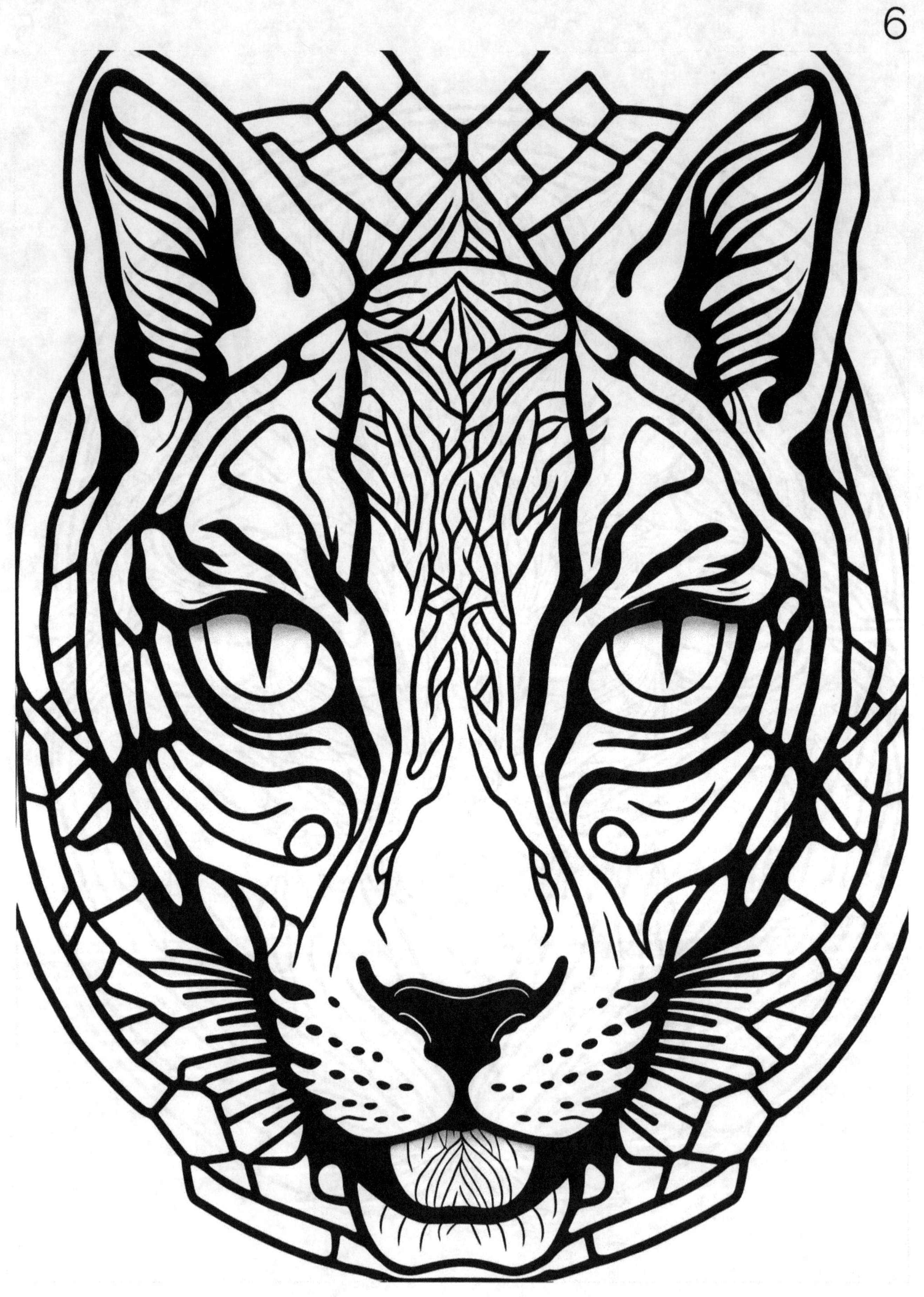

Asian leopard

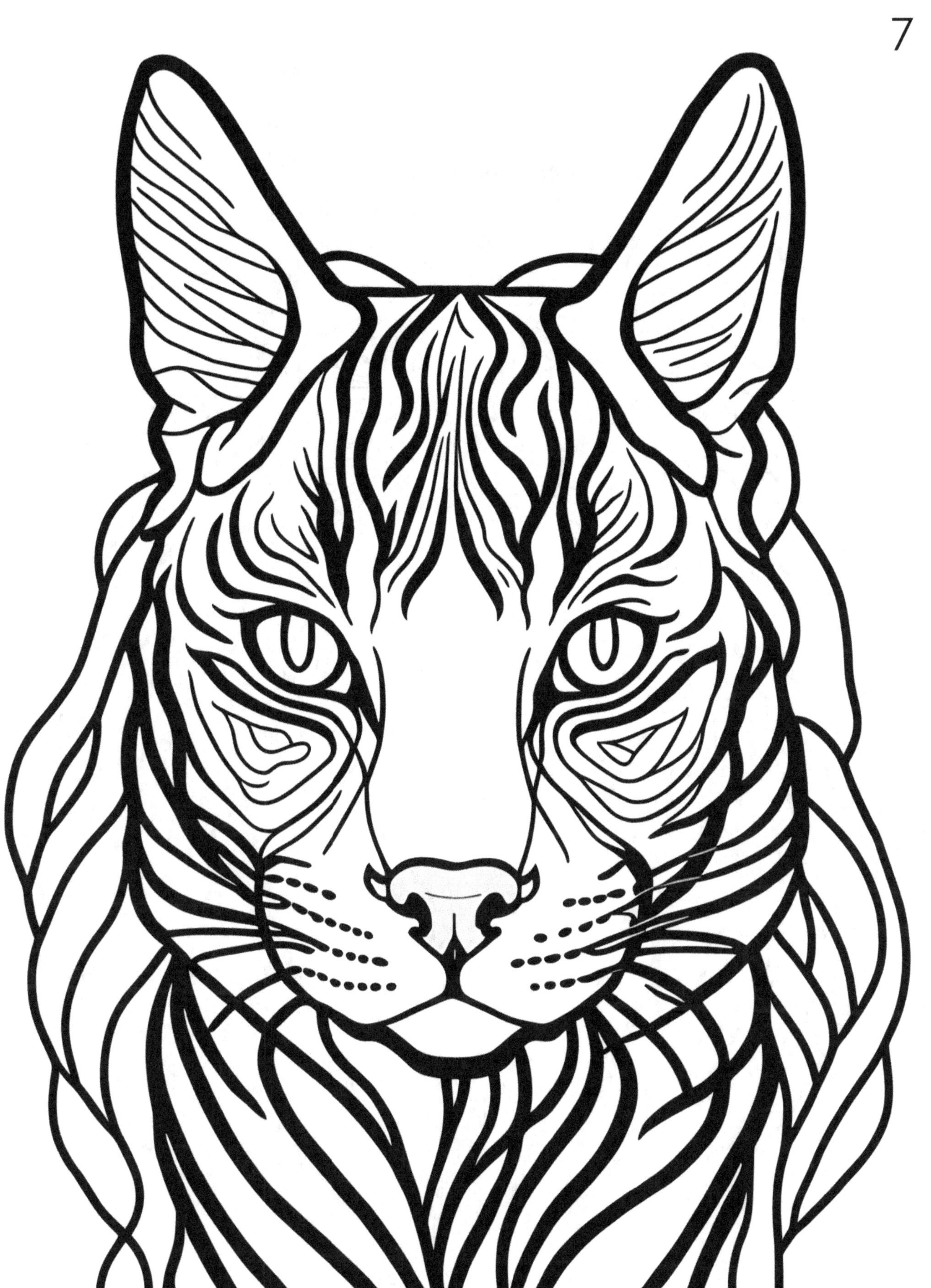

Bengal cat

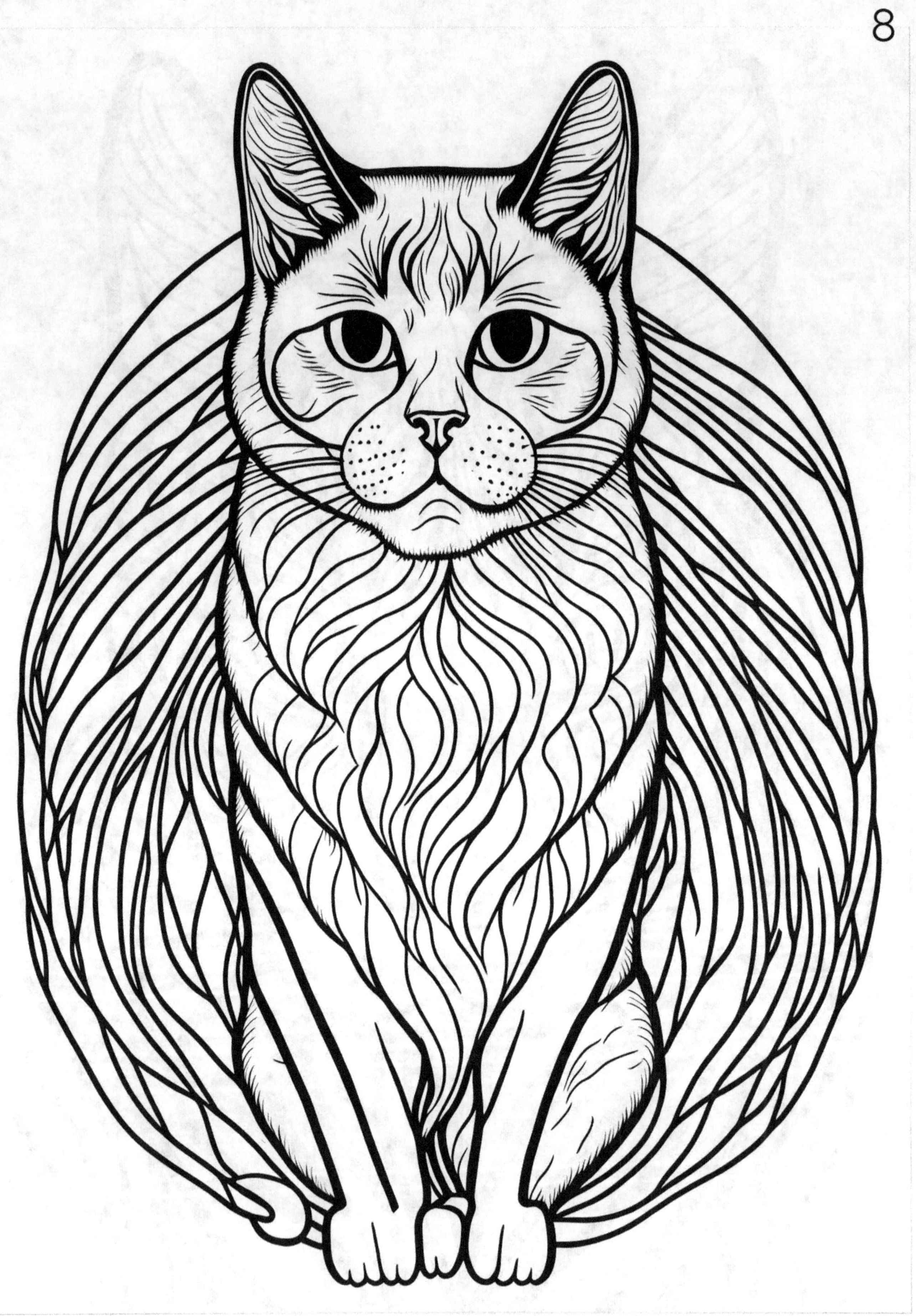

Birman bobtail

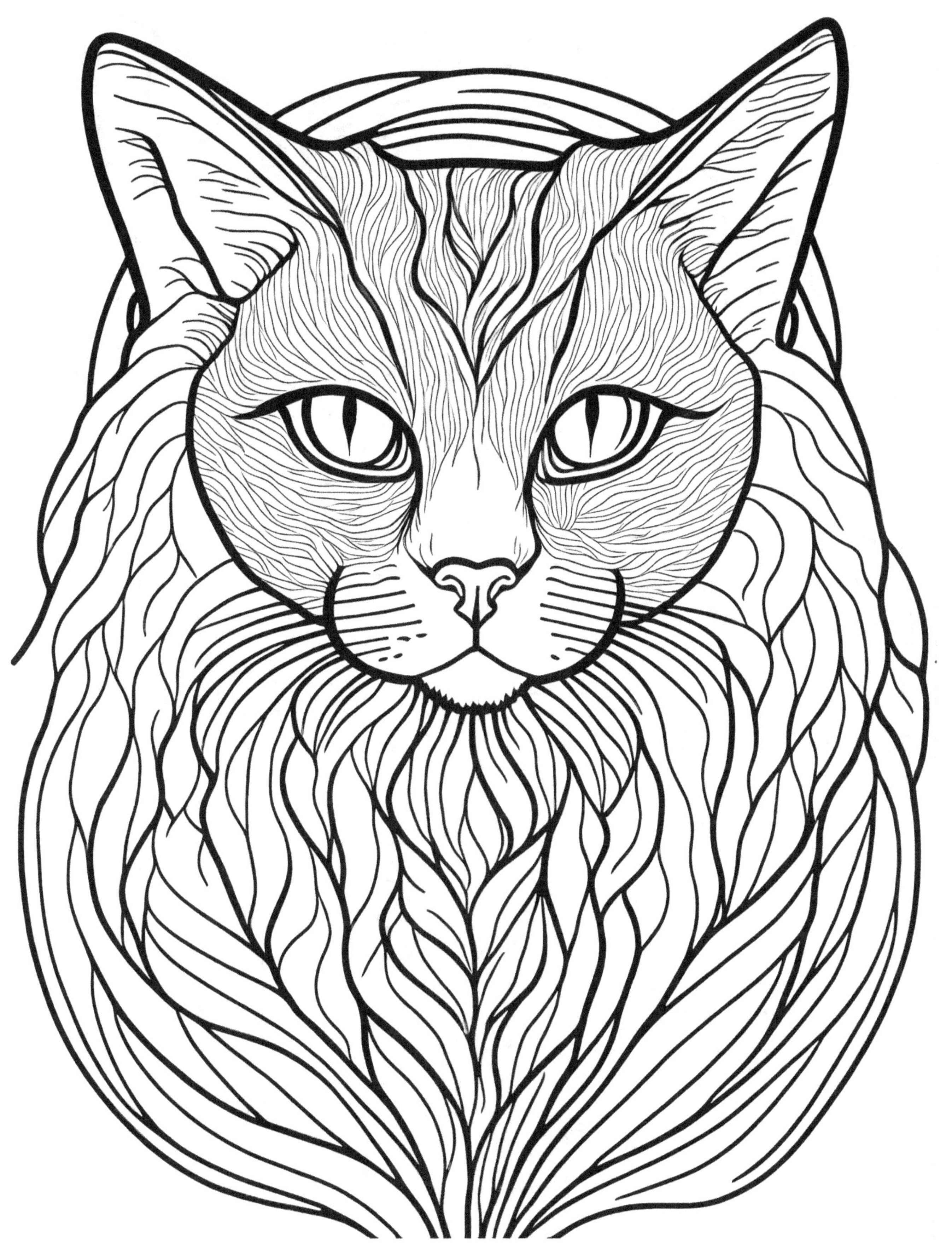

Bombay bobtail cat

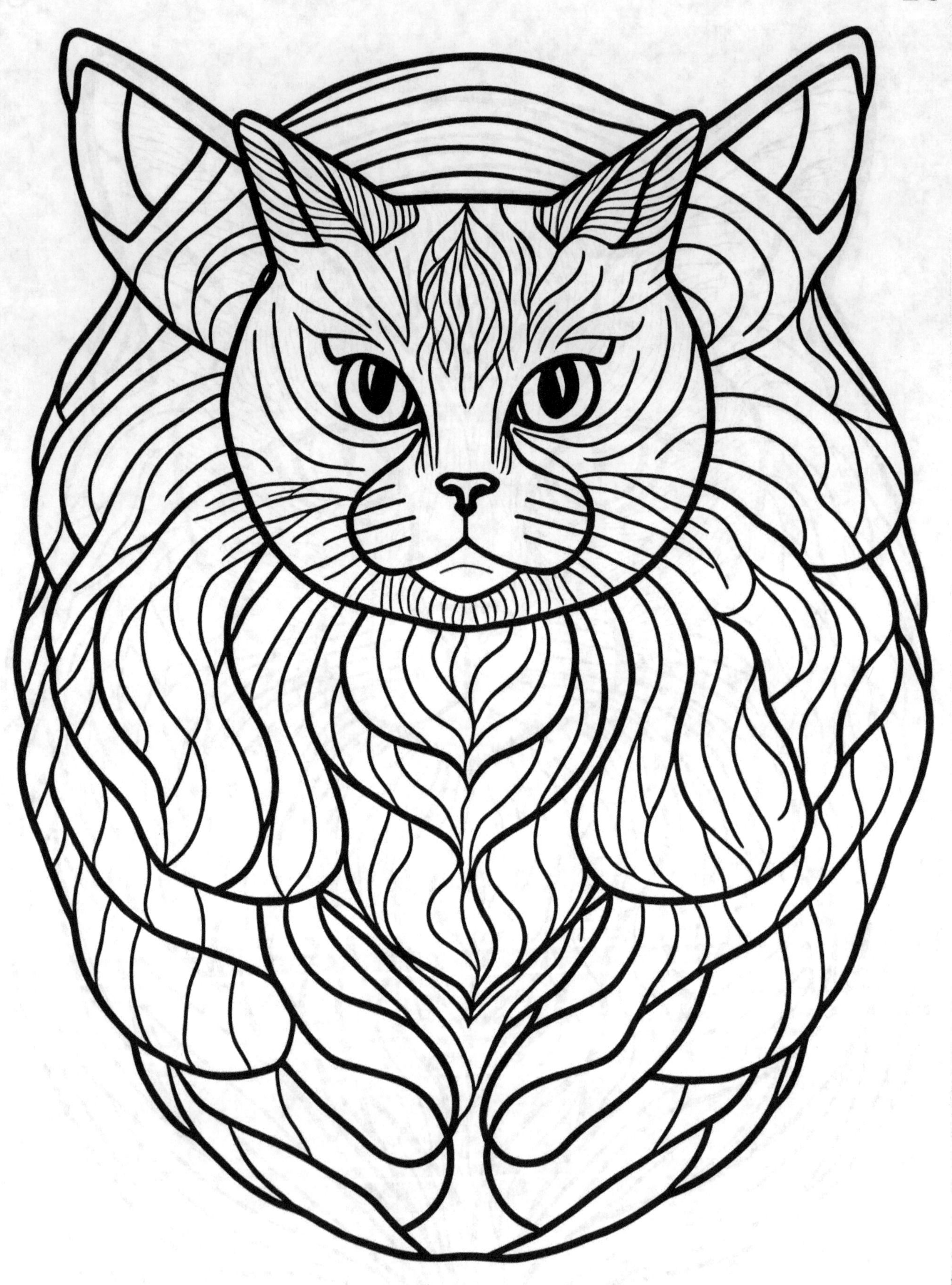

Burmilla bobtail cat

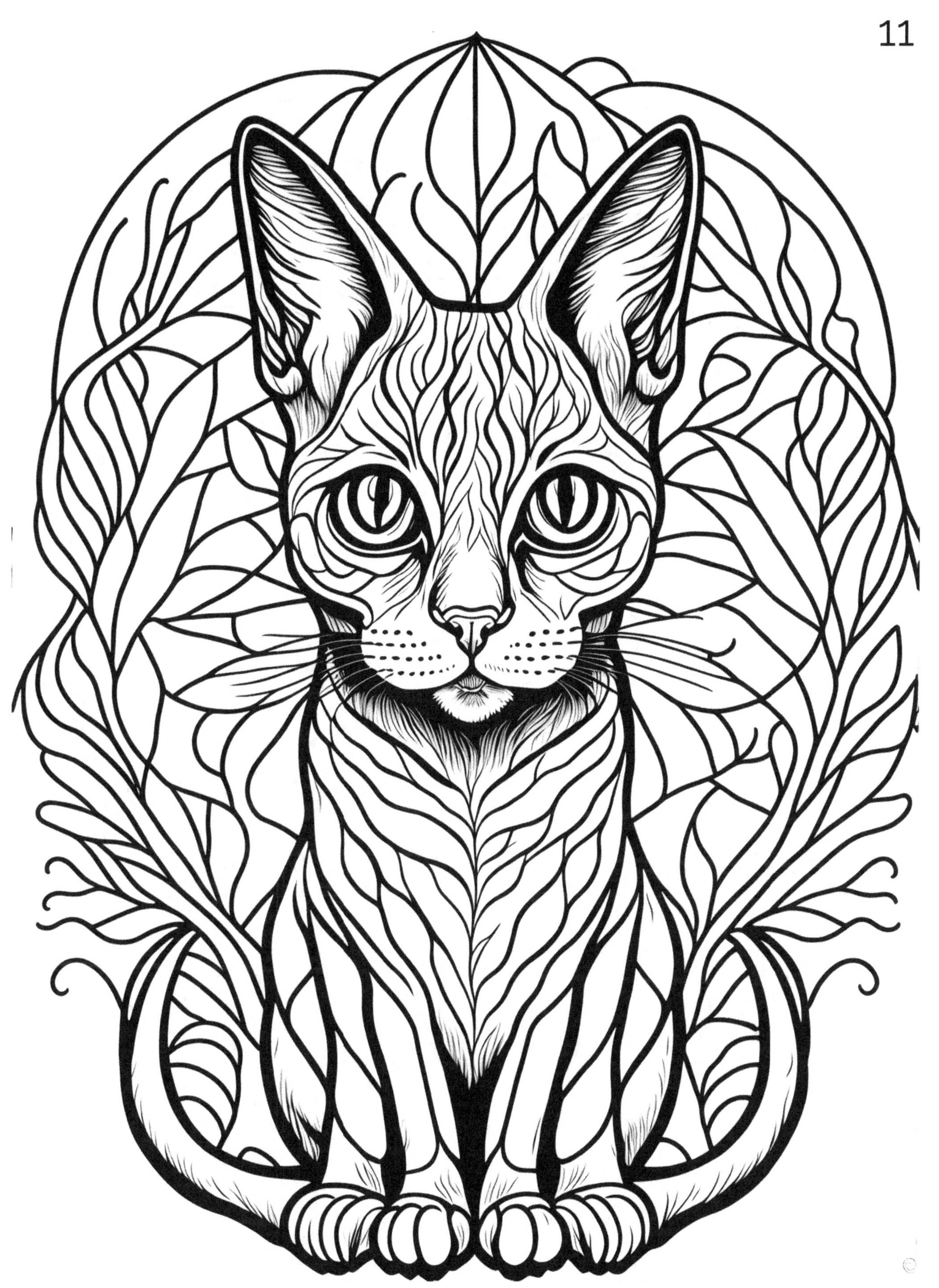

Devon Rex bobtail cat

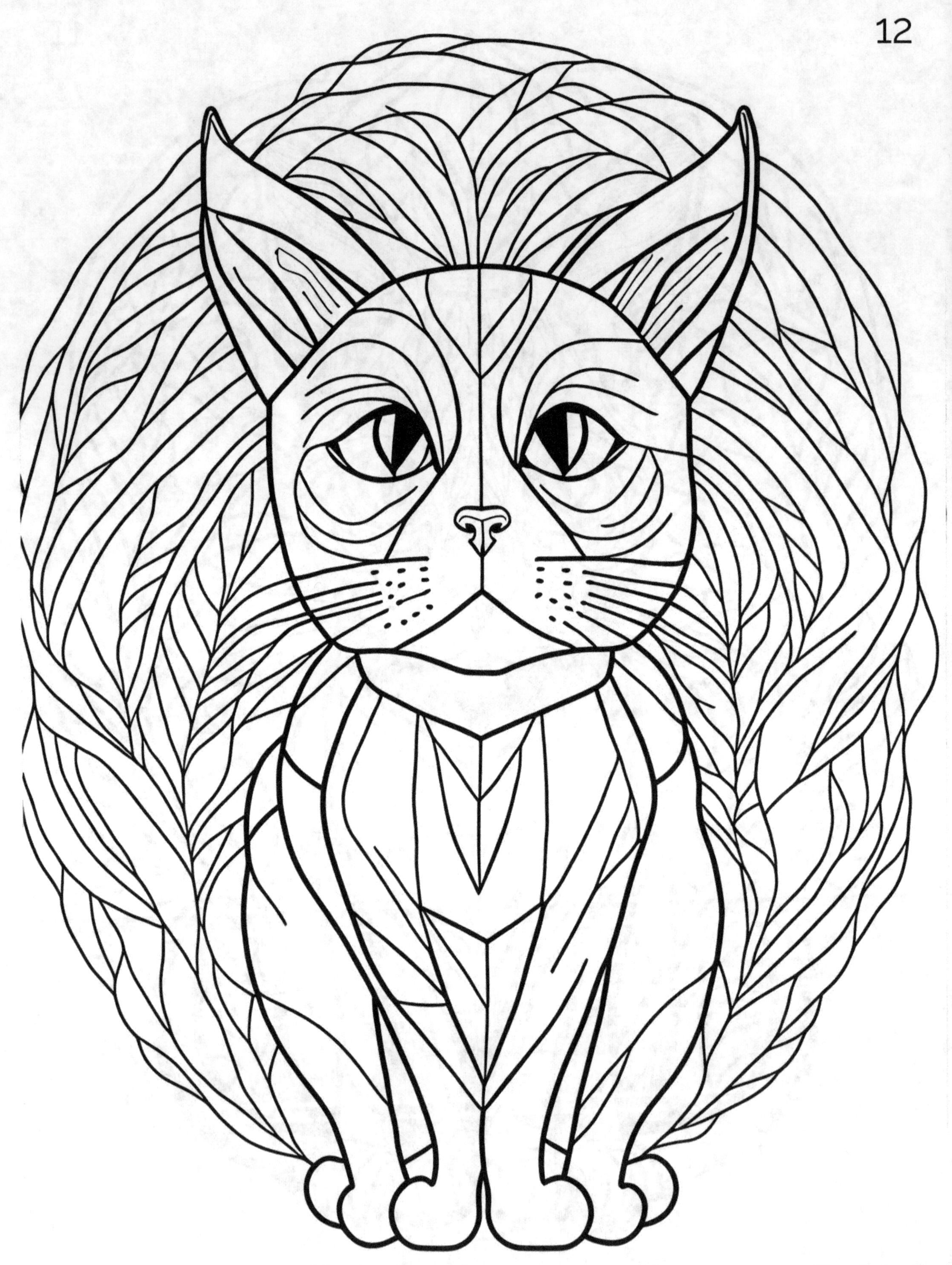

Japanese Bobtail

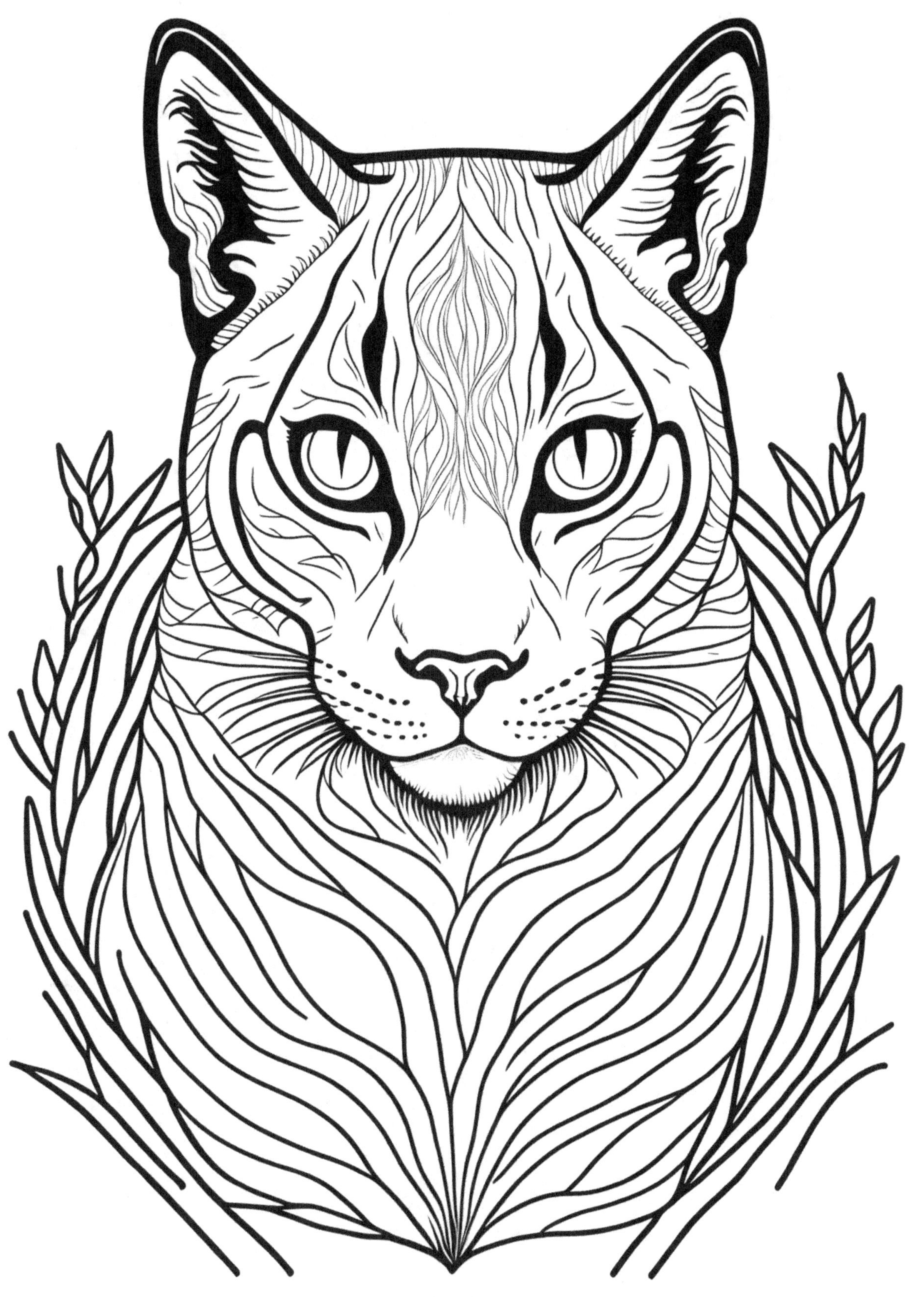

Kalahari desert cat

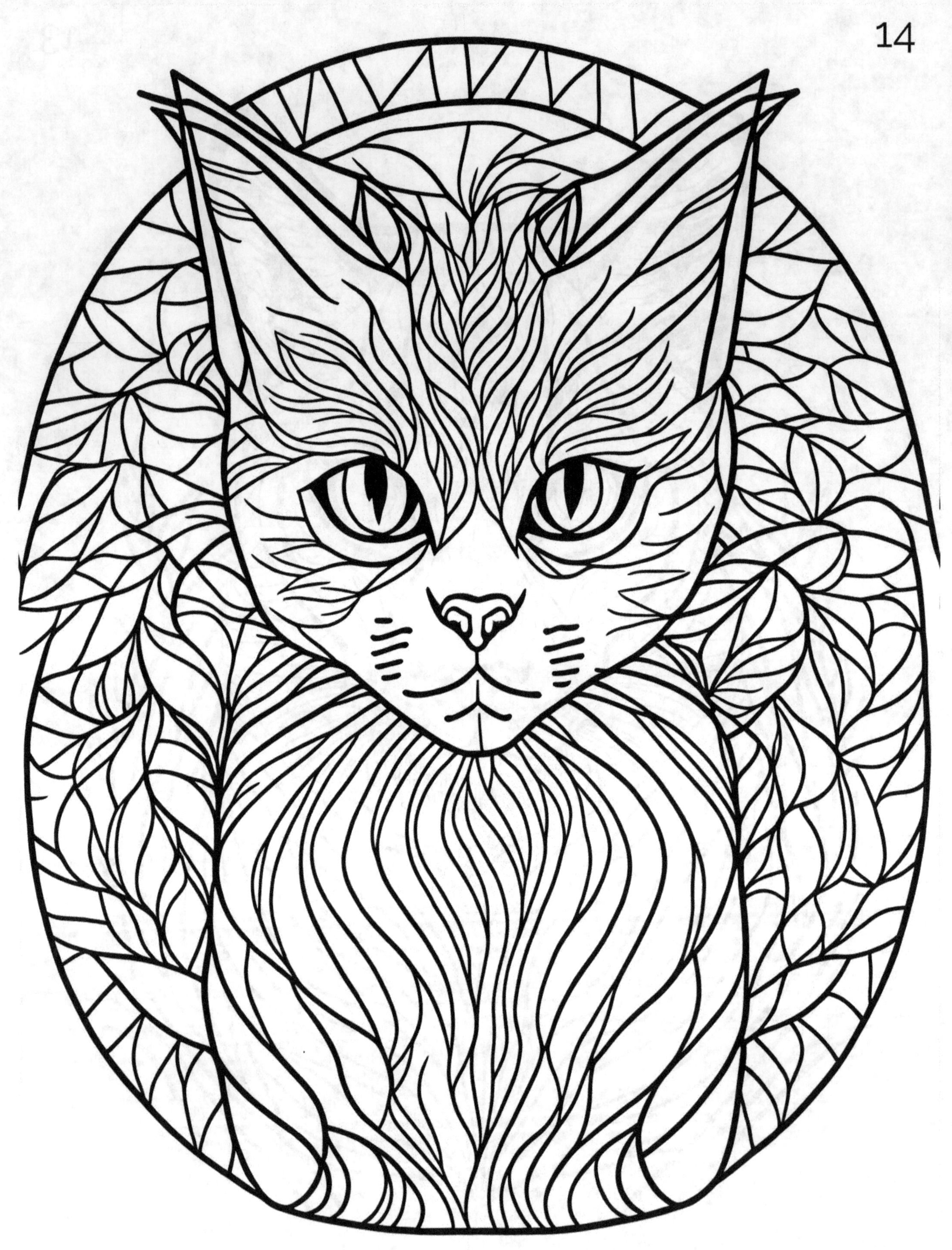

Kinkalow bobtail cat

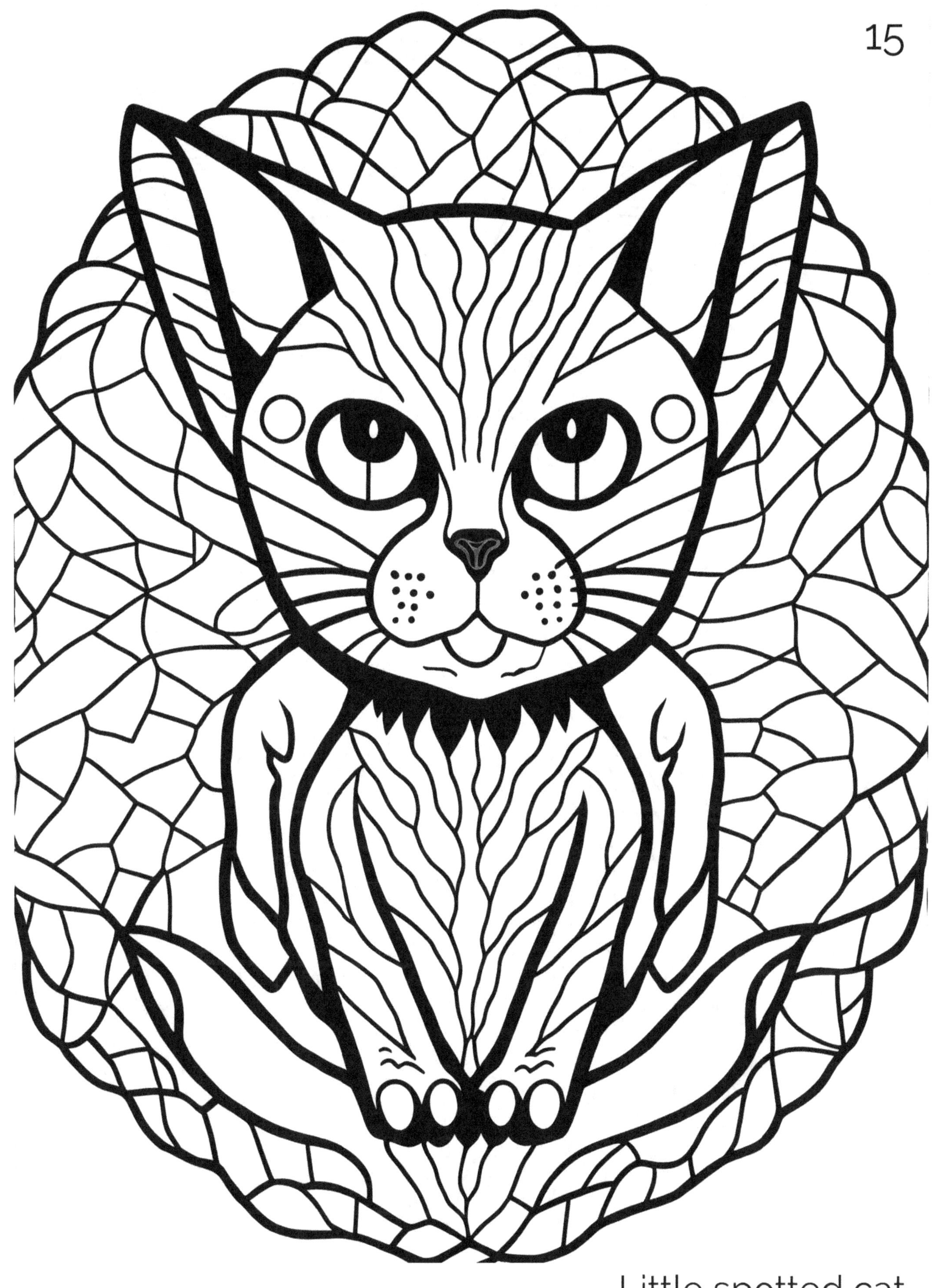

Little spotted cat

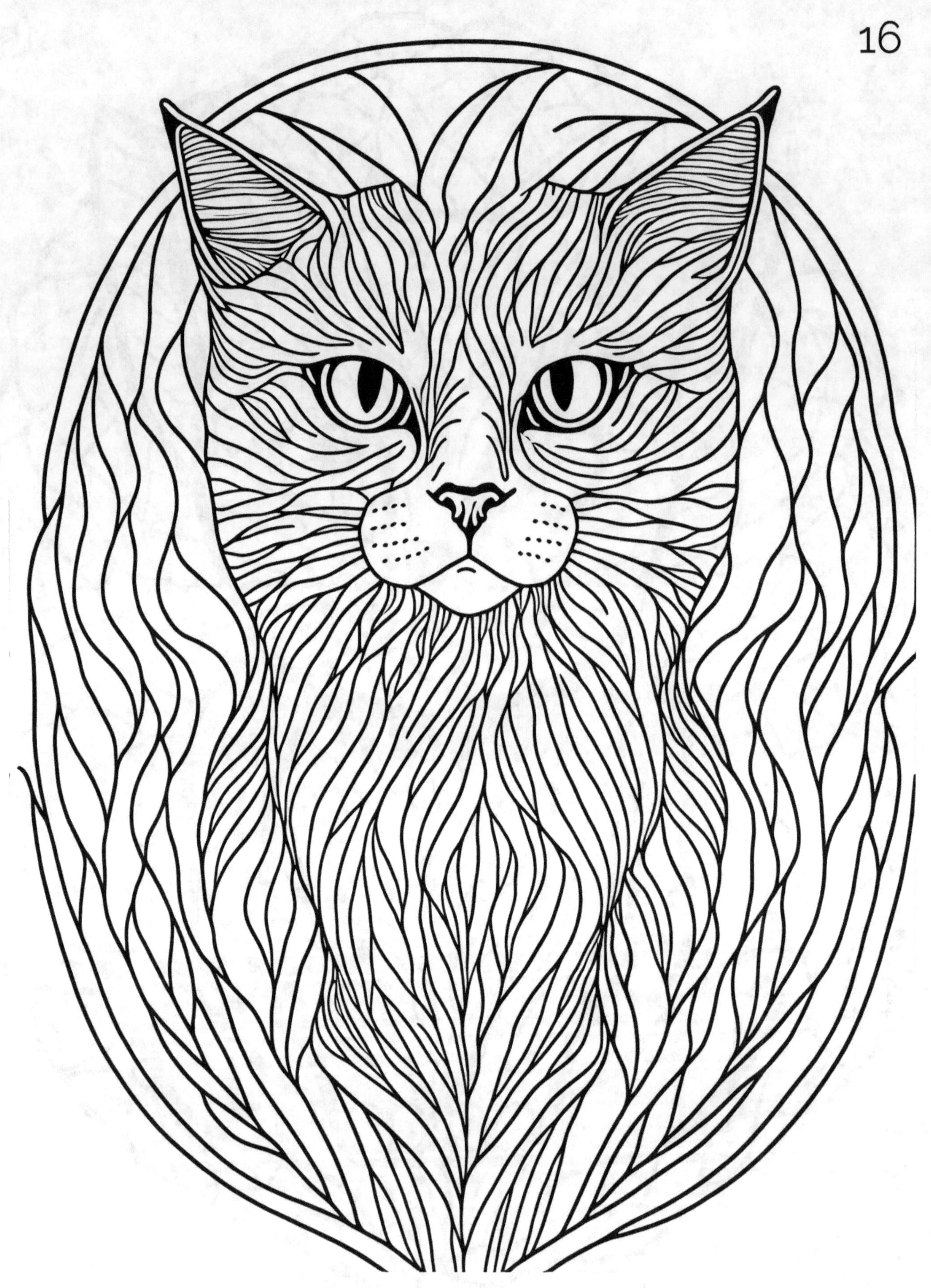

Manx bobtail cat

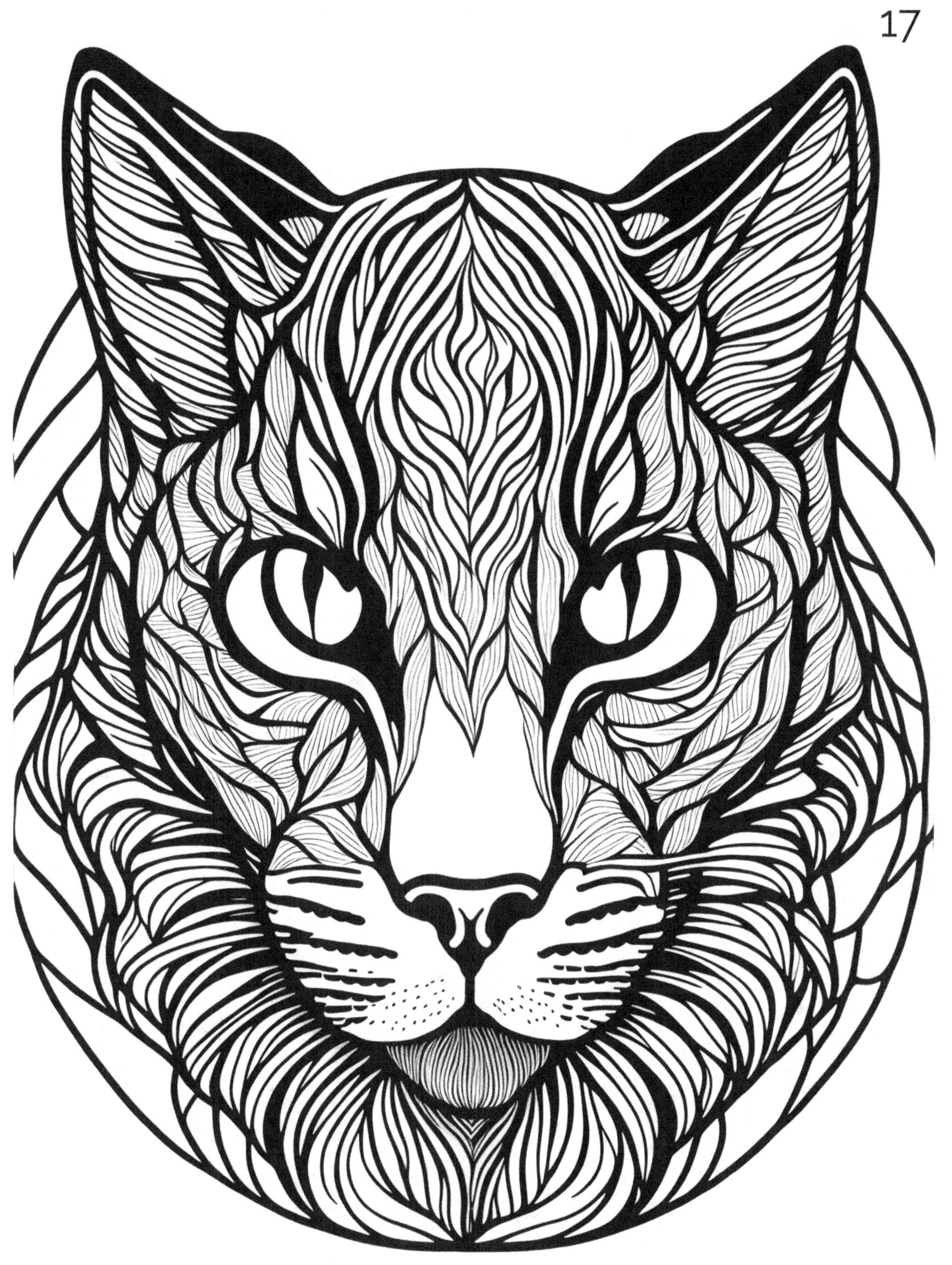

Marbled cat

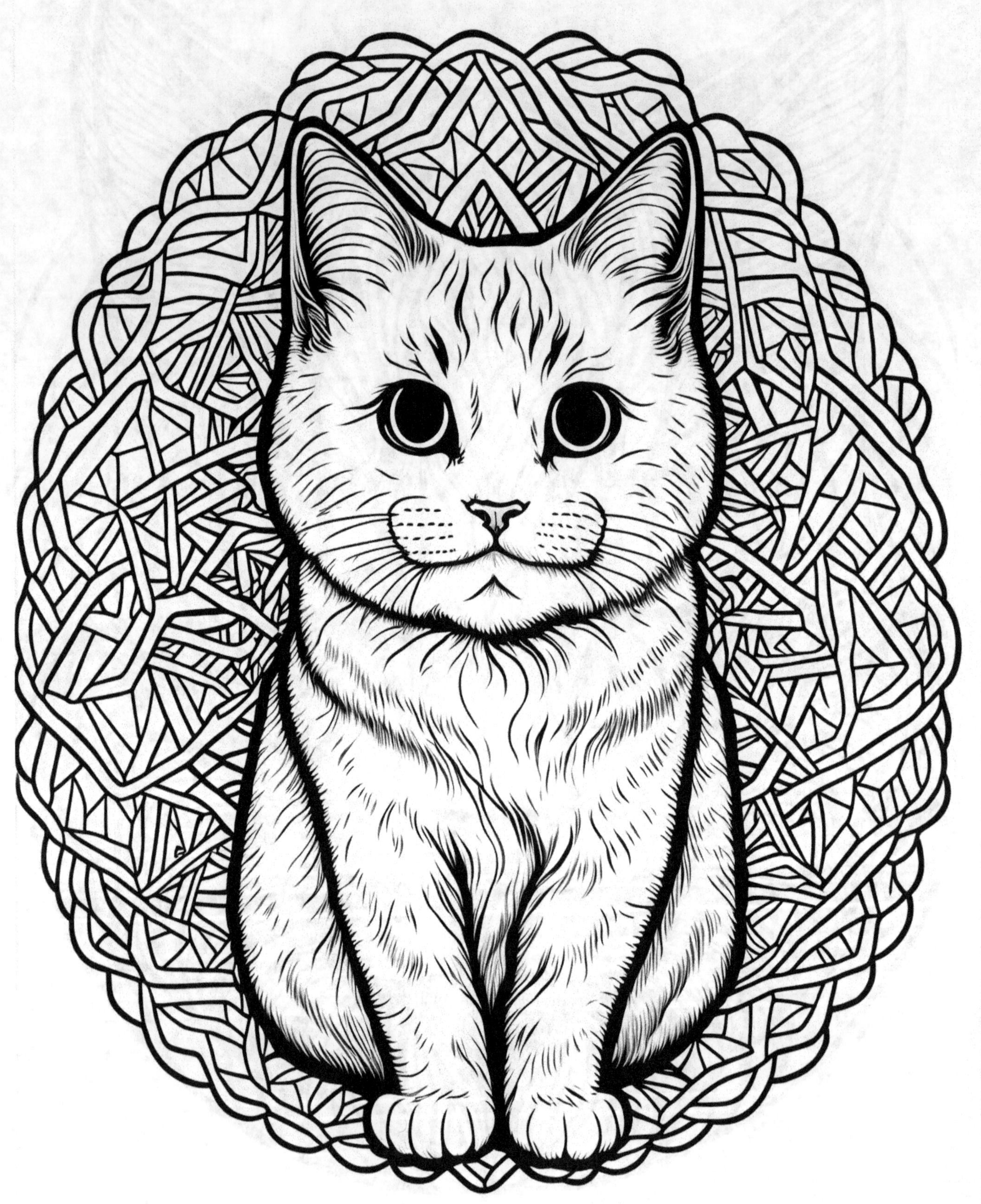

Munchkin Bobtail Cat

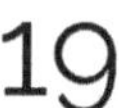

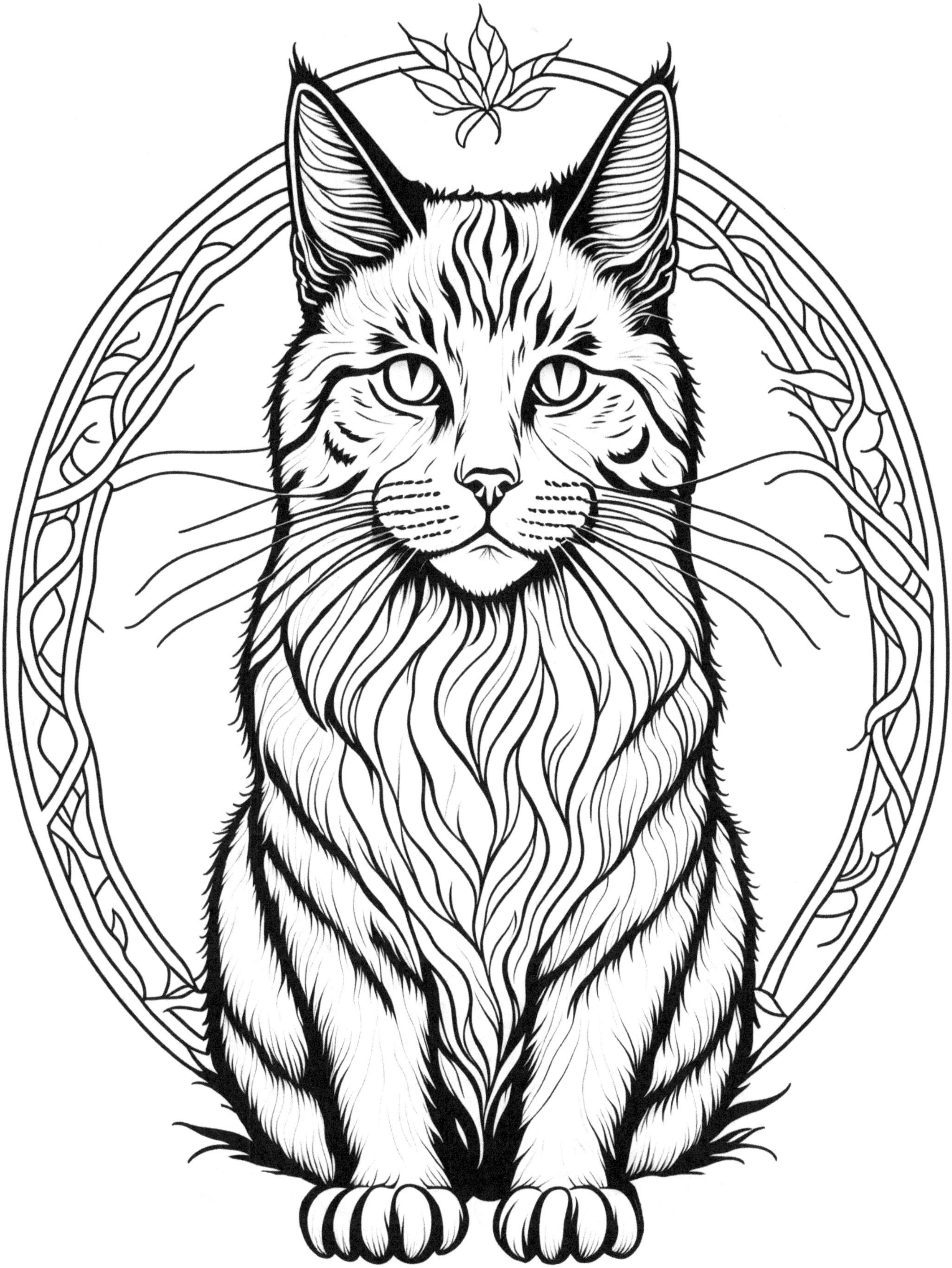

Norwegian Forest bobtail cat

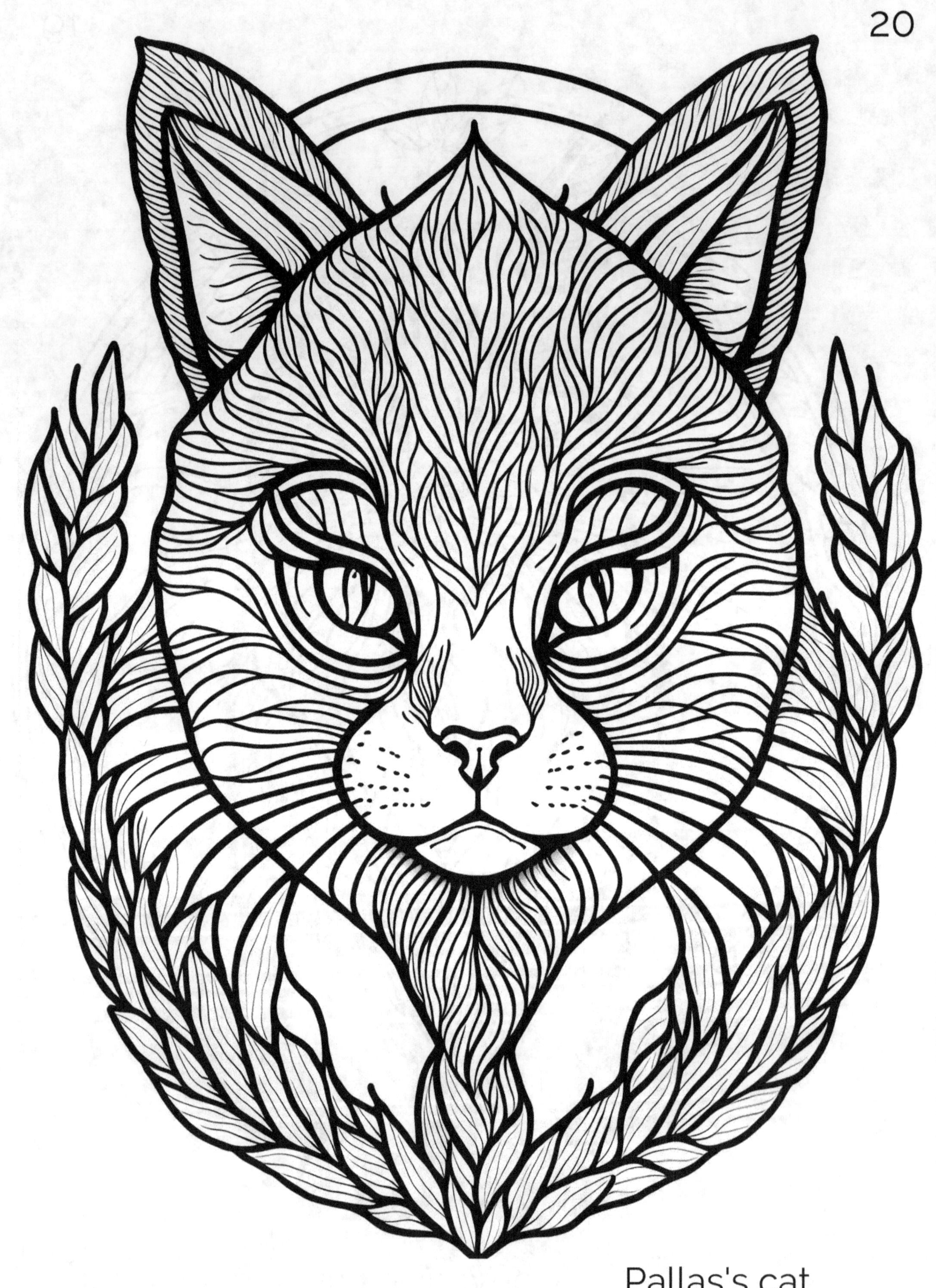

Pallas's cat

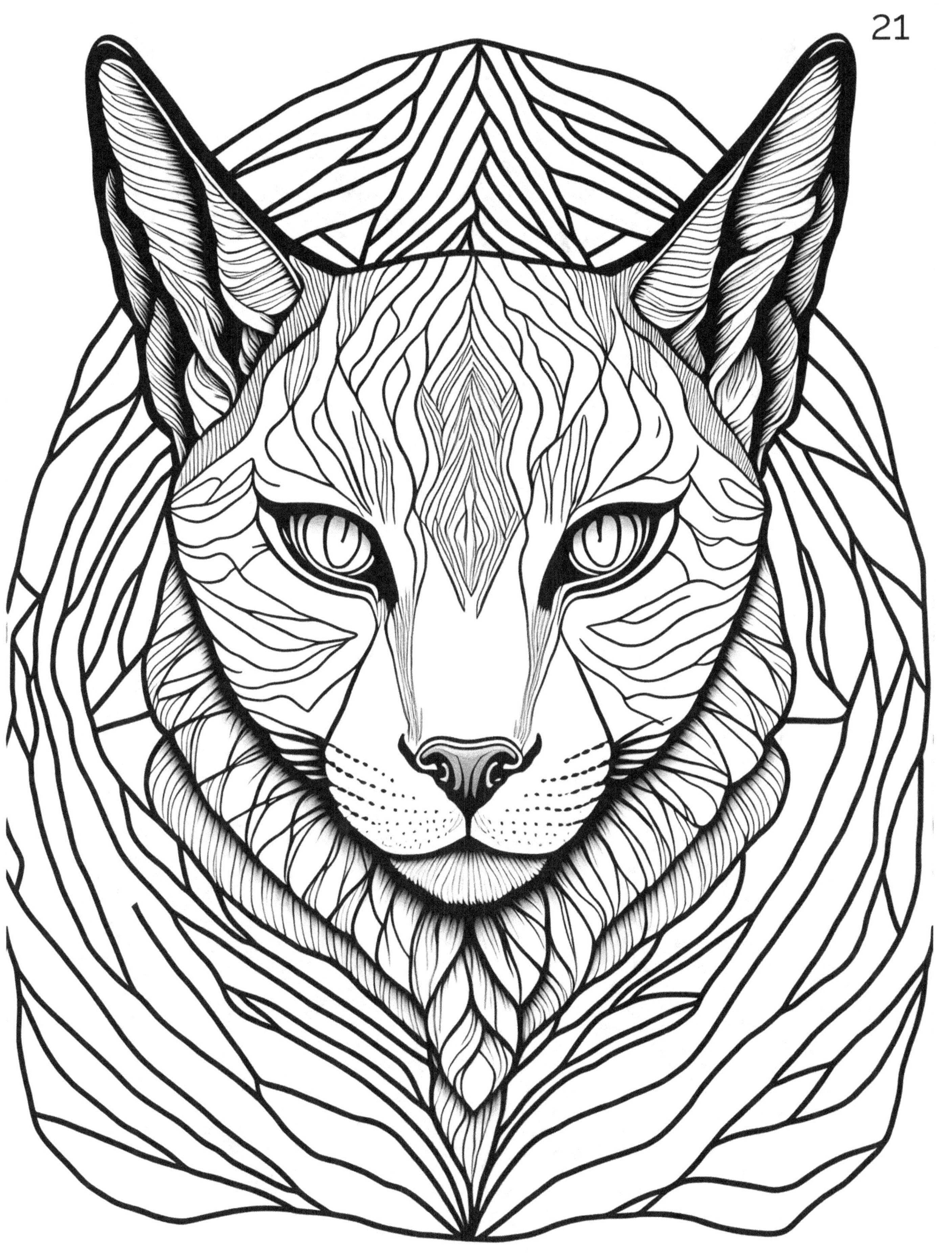

Pallas's desert cat

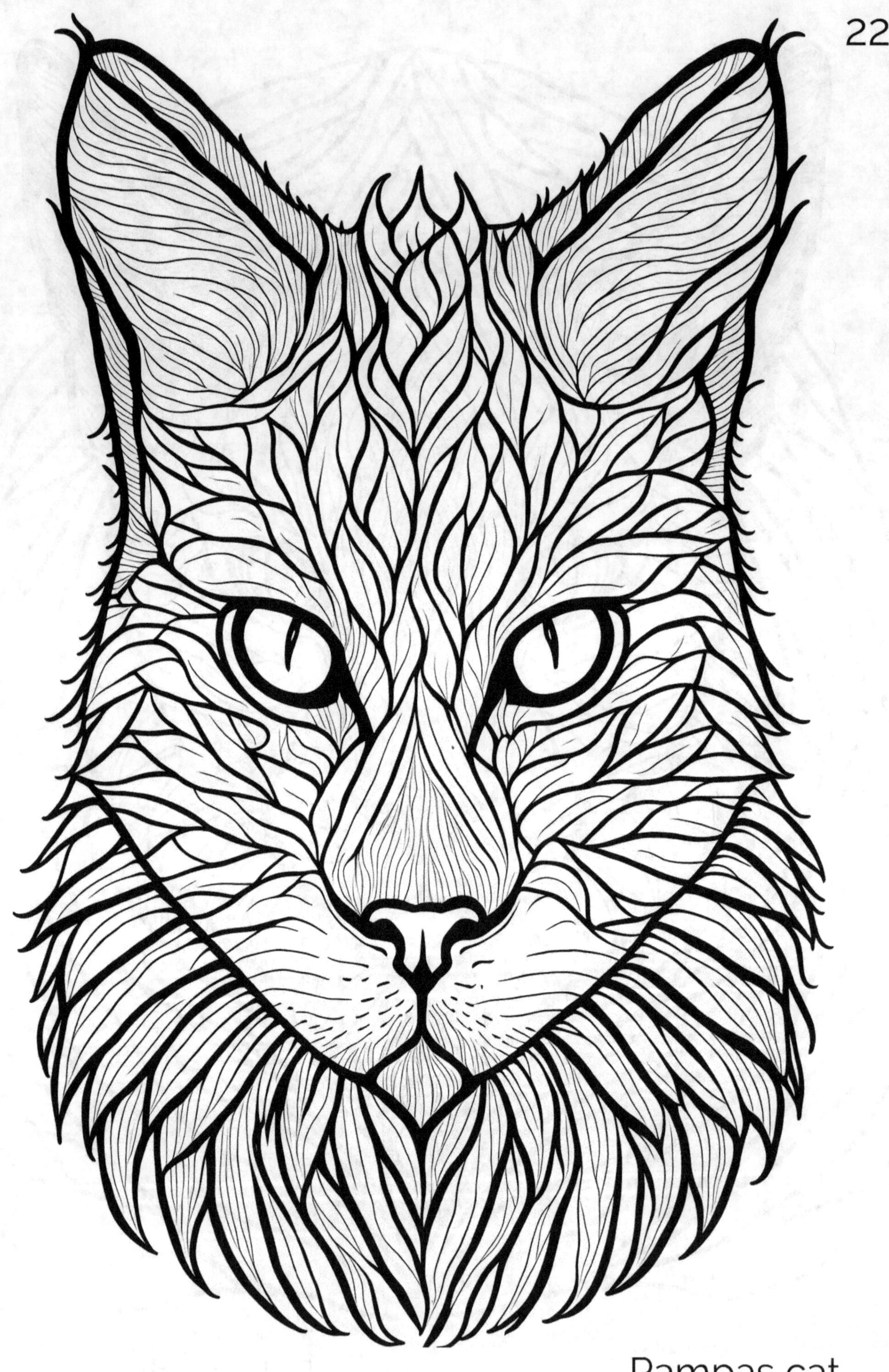

Pampas cat

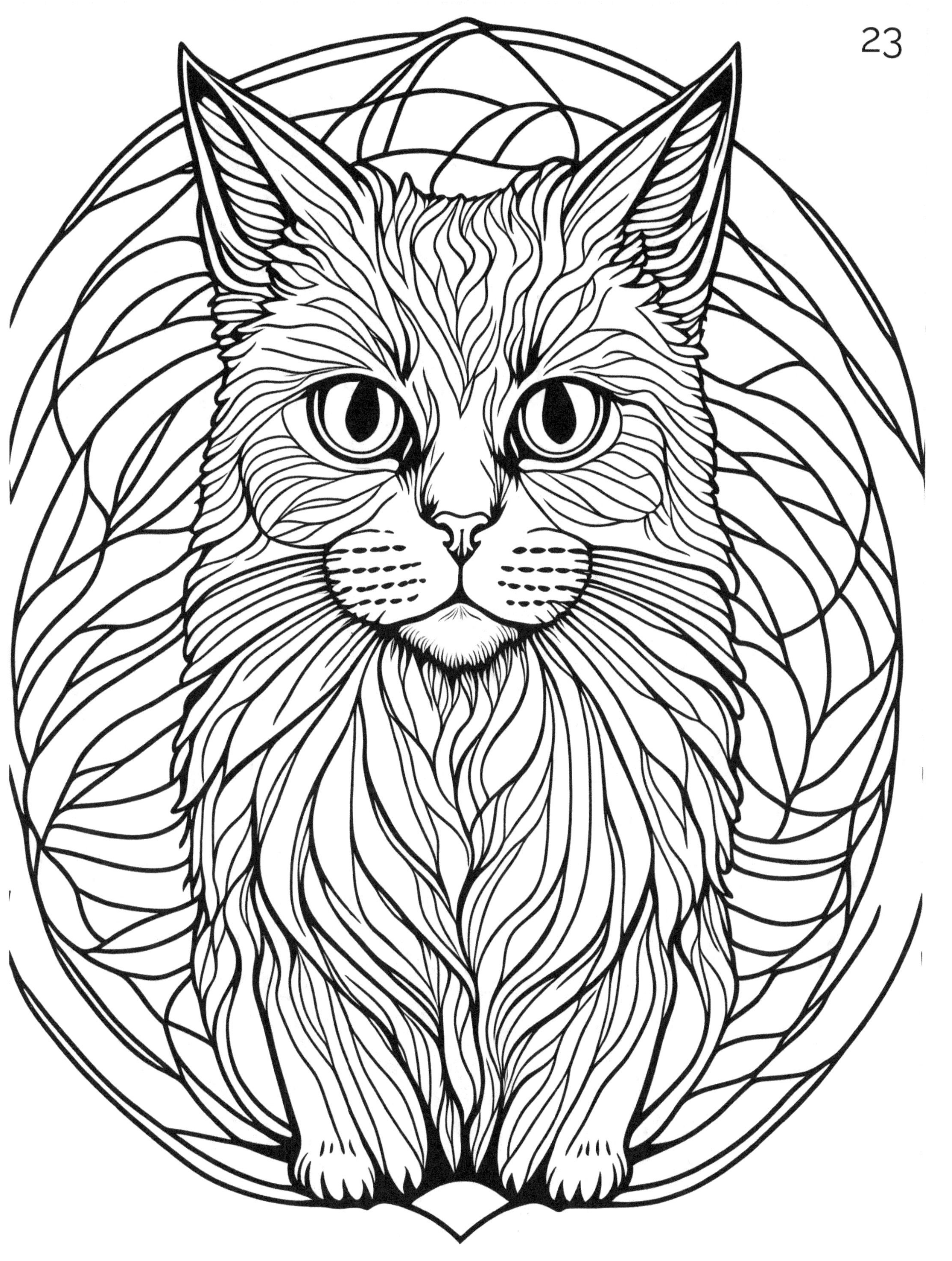

Persian bobtail

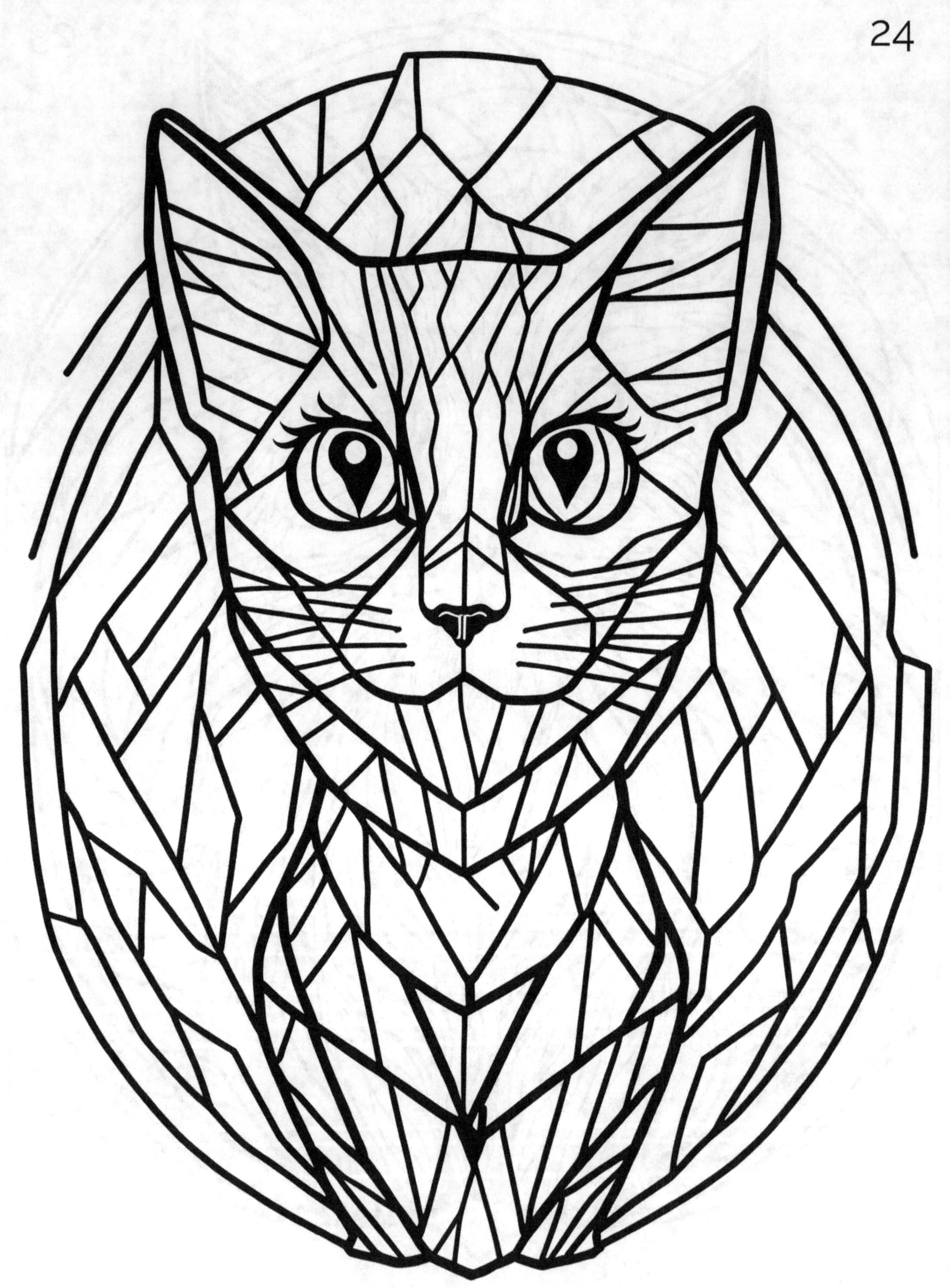

Pixiebob bobtail cat

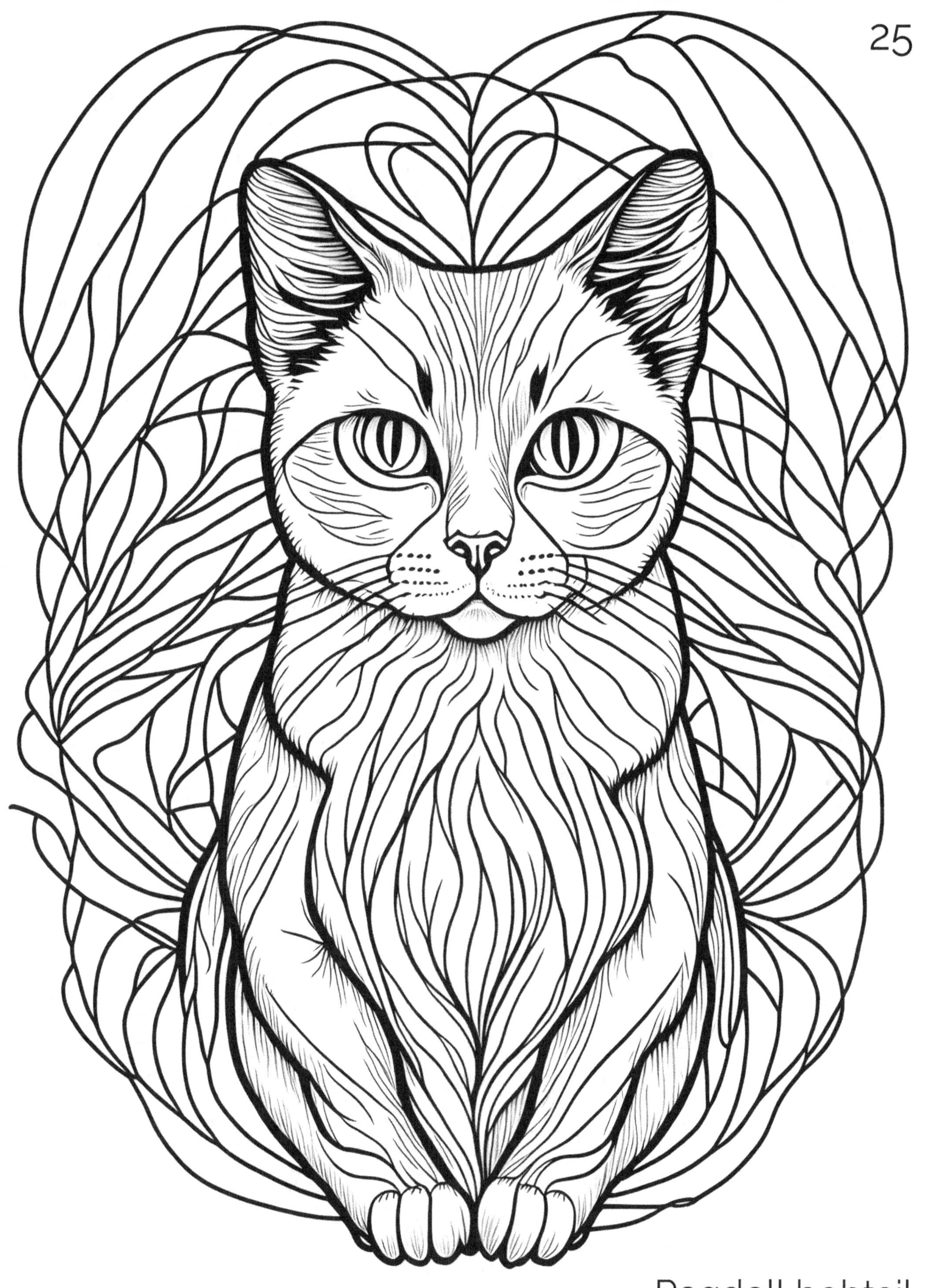

Ragdoll bobtail

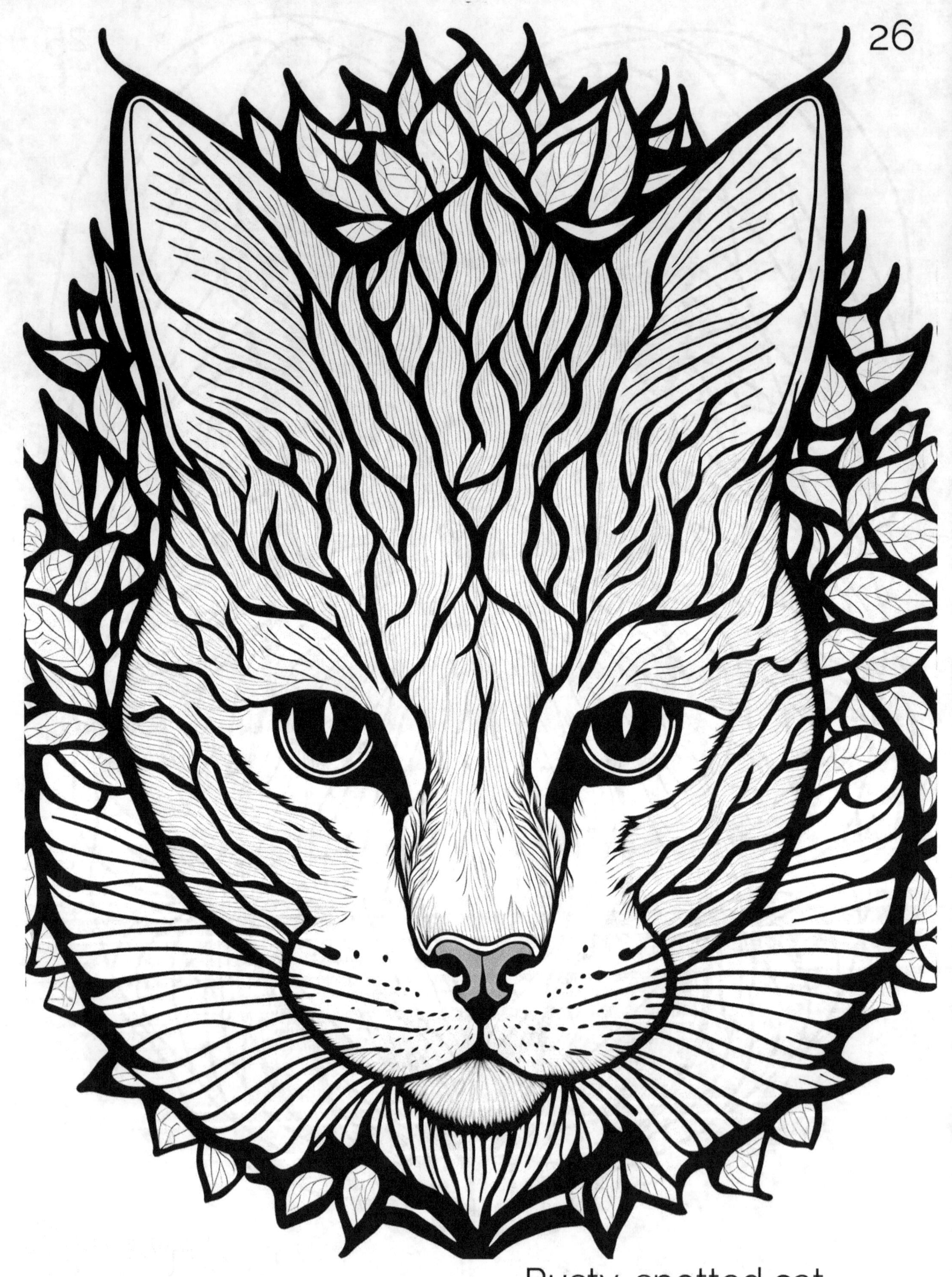

Rusty-spotted cat

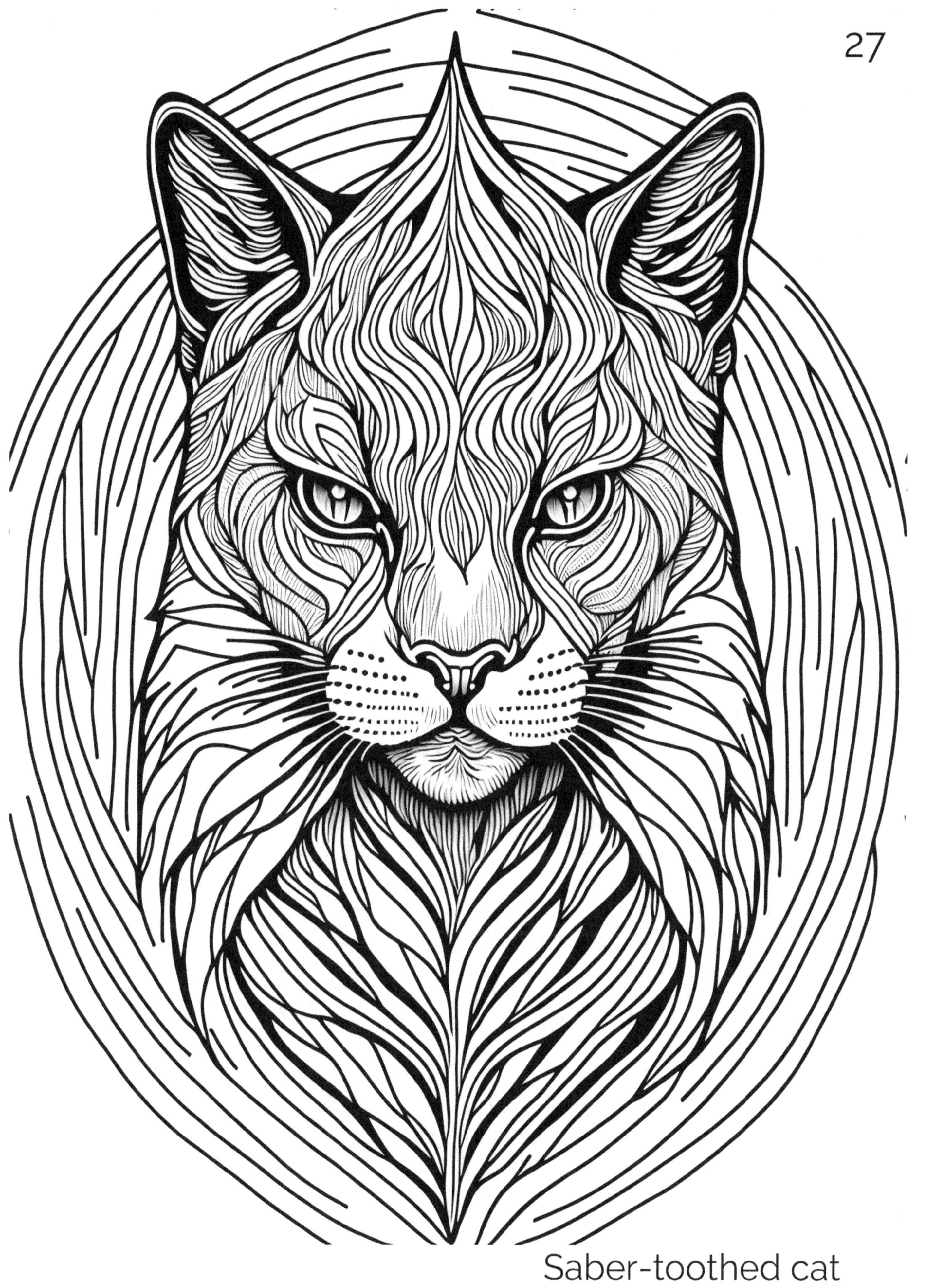

Saber-toothed cat

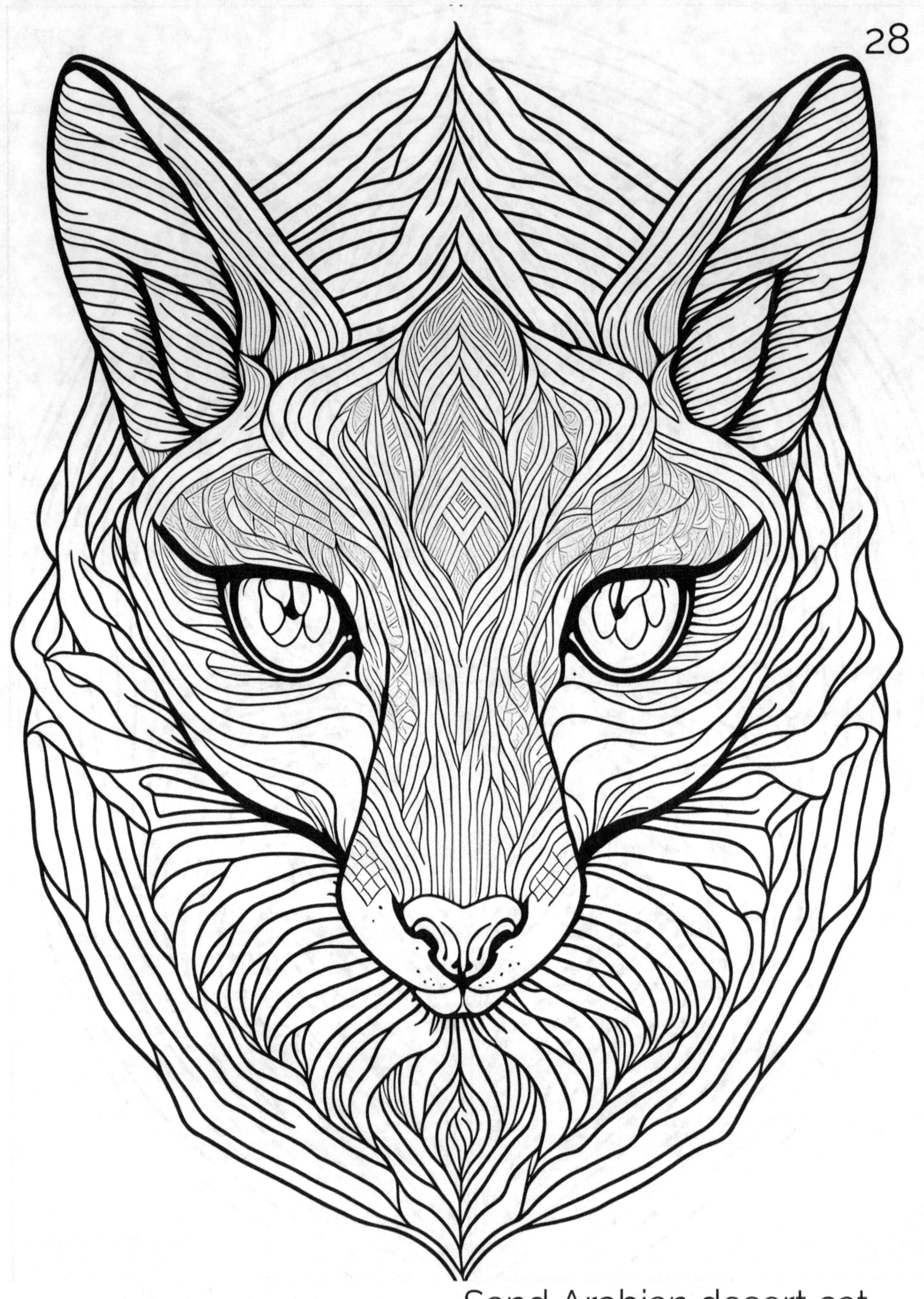

Sand Arabian desert cat

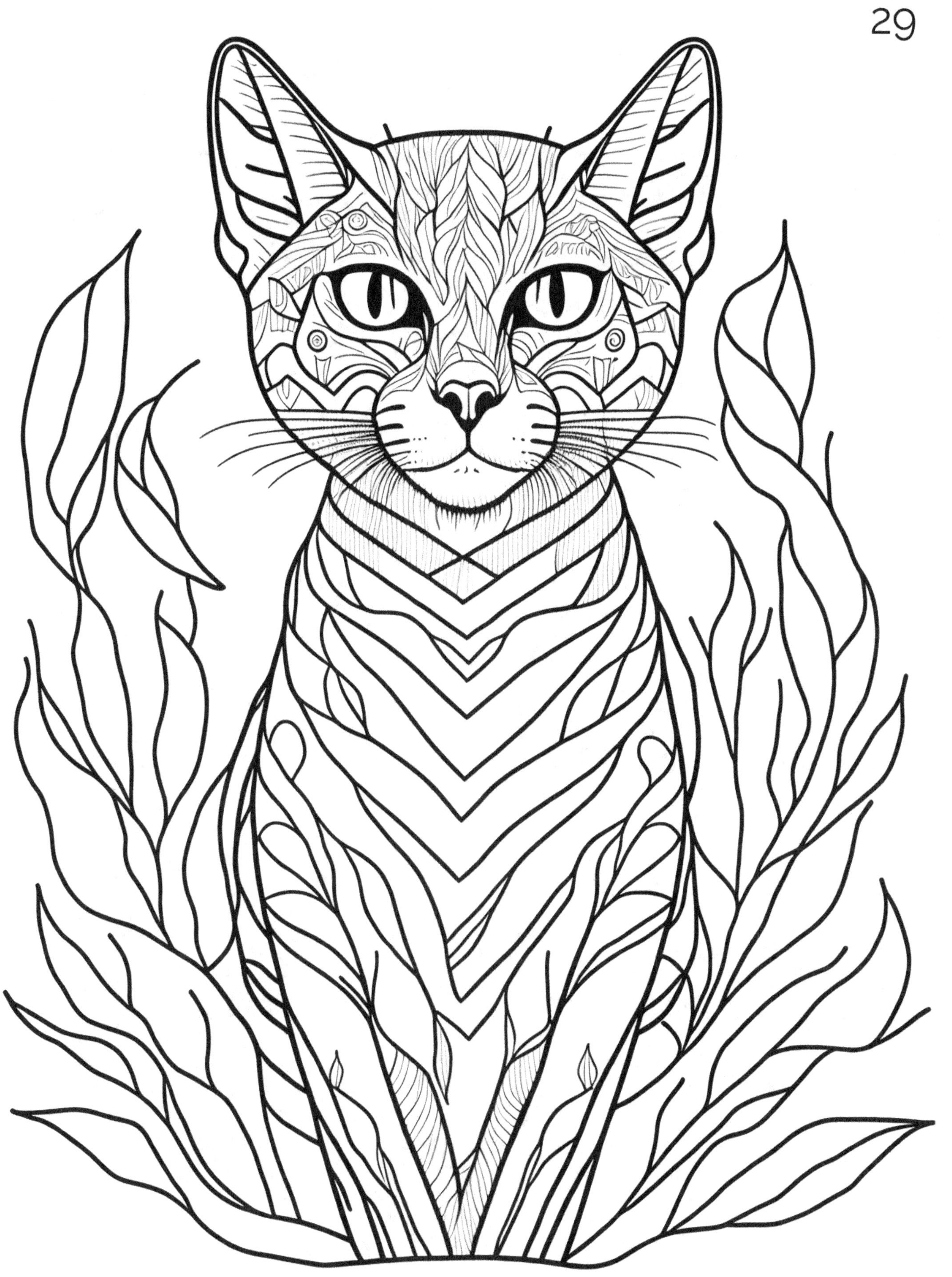

Sand cat

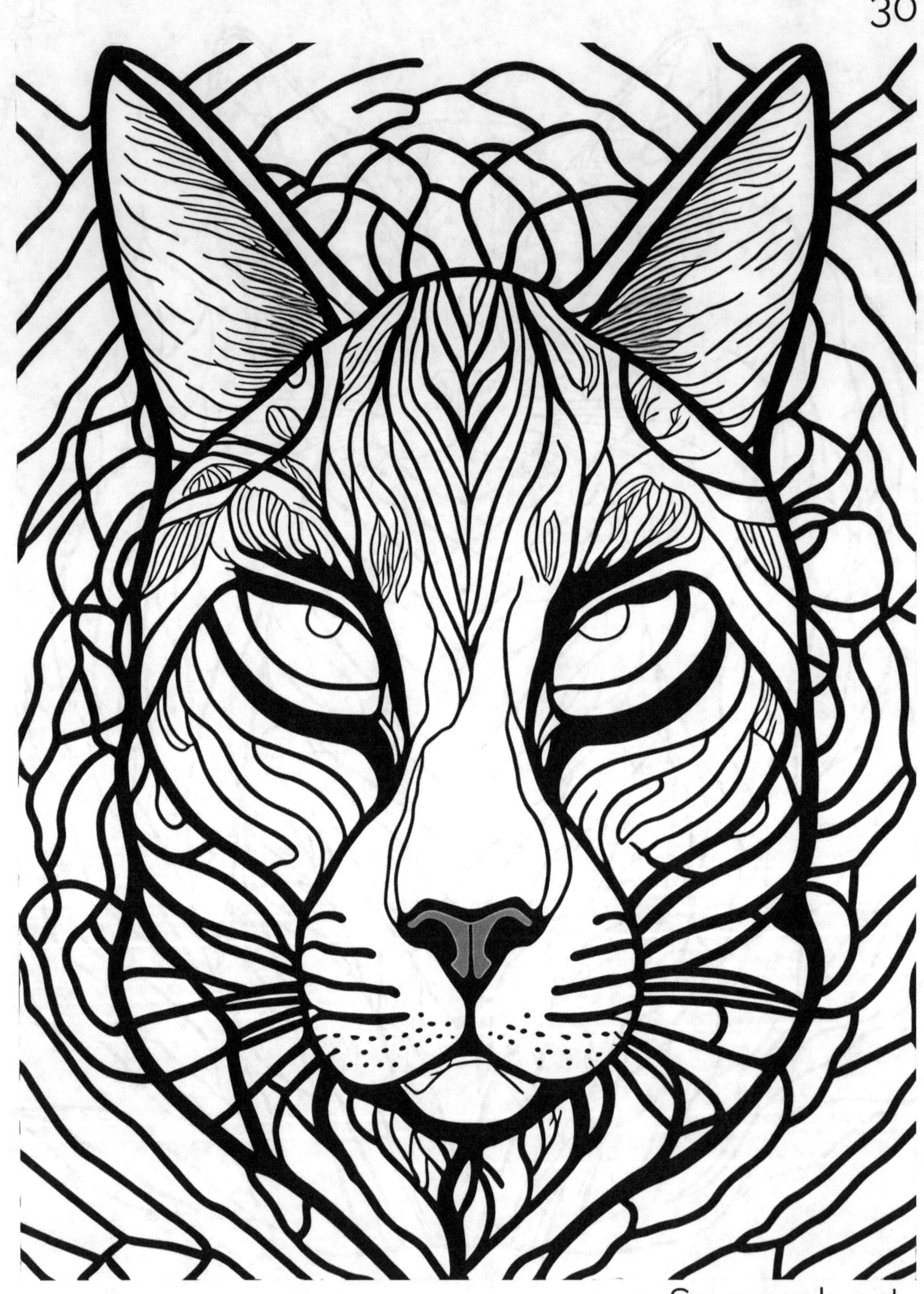

Savannah cat

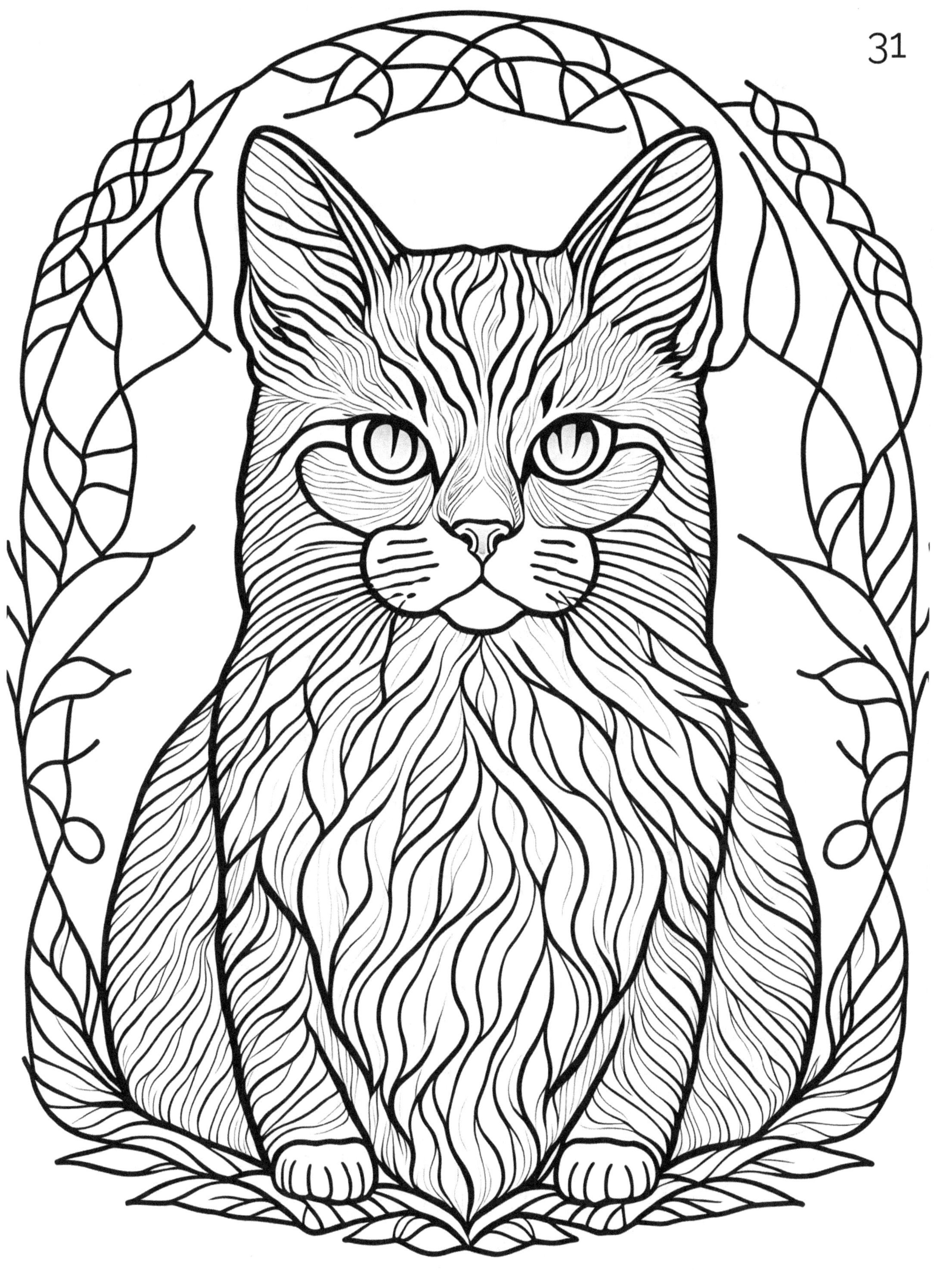

Selkirk Rex

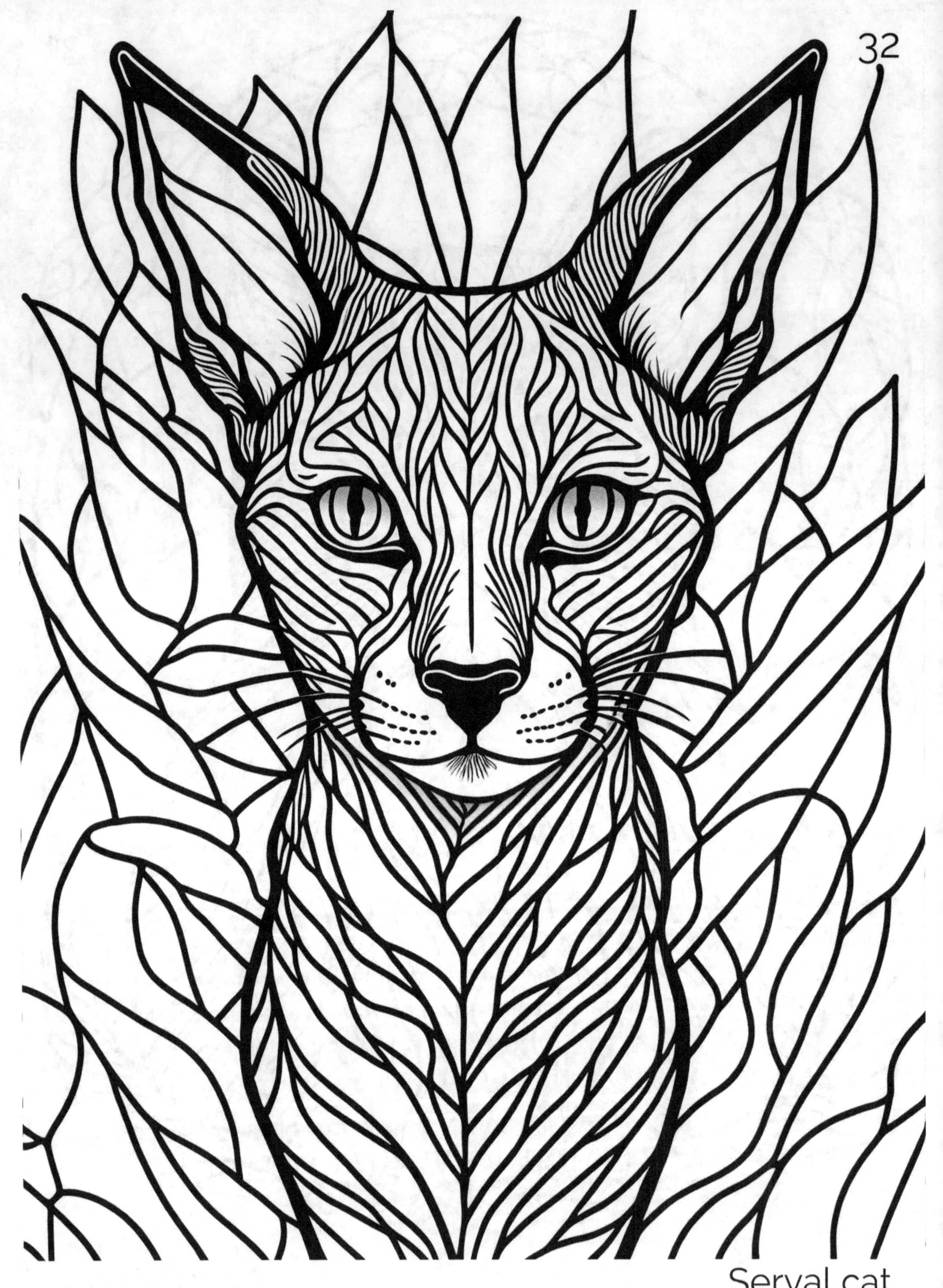

Serval cat

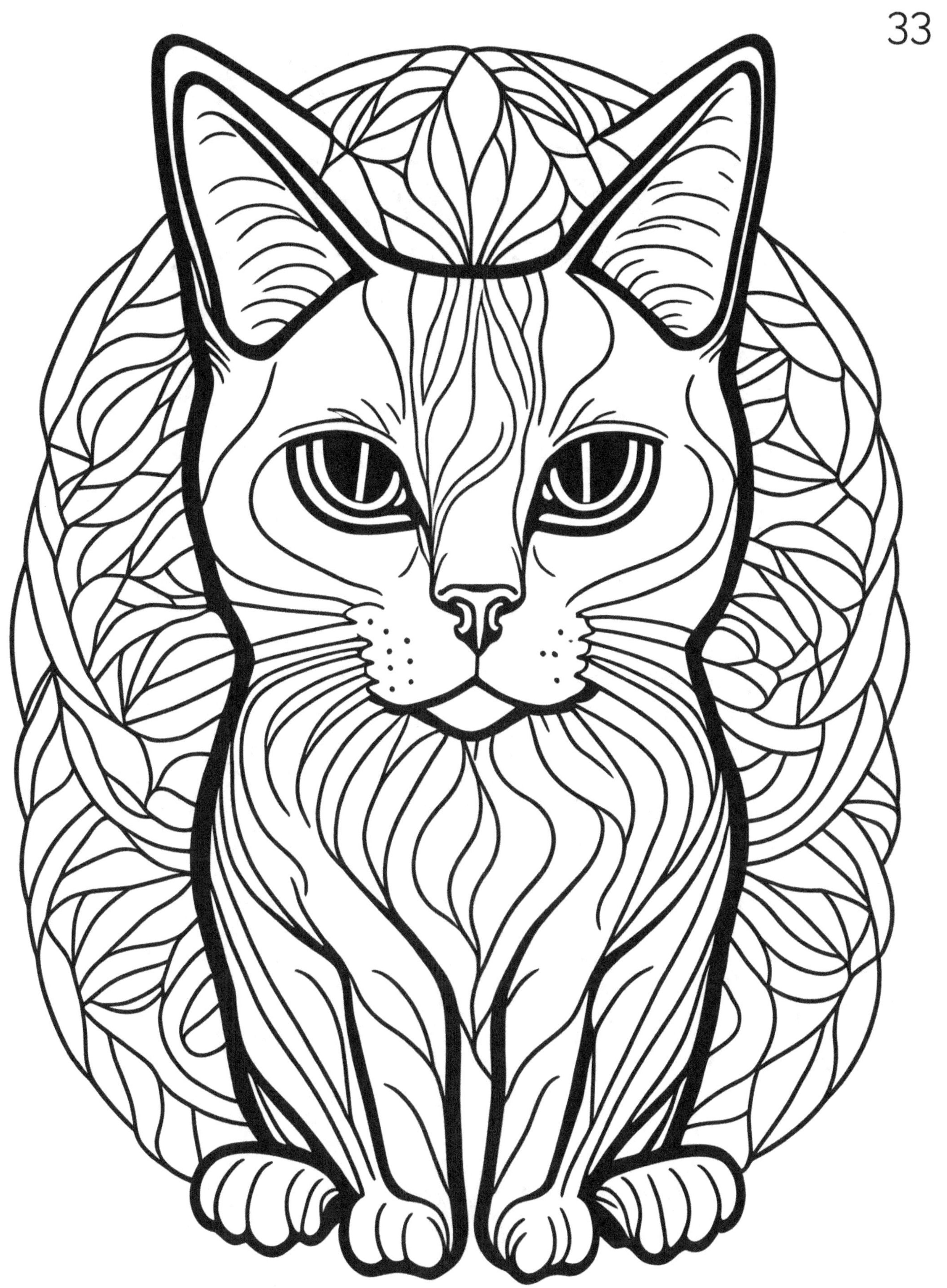

Siamese bobtail cat

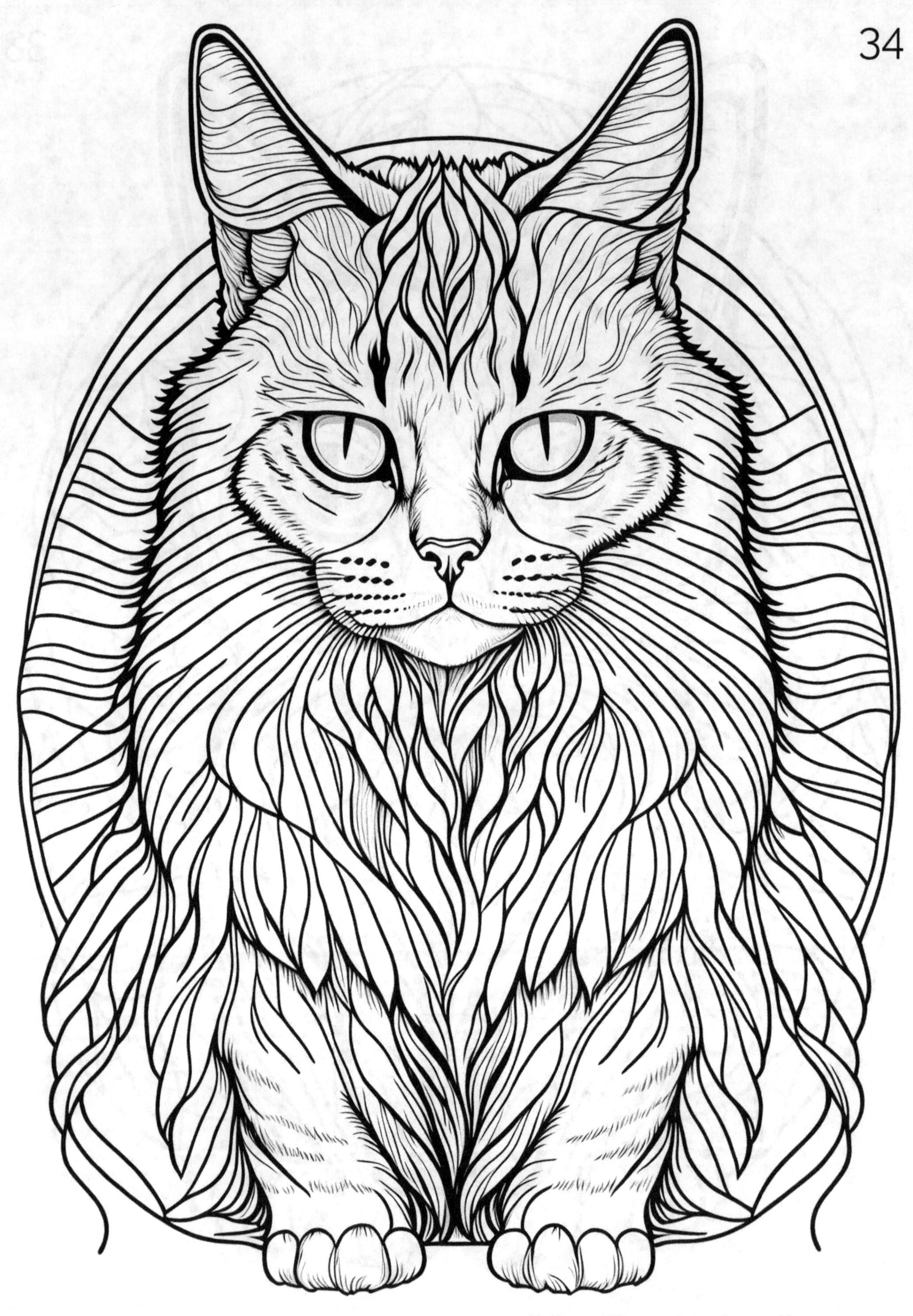

Siberian bobtail cat

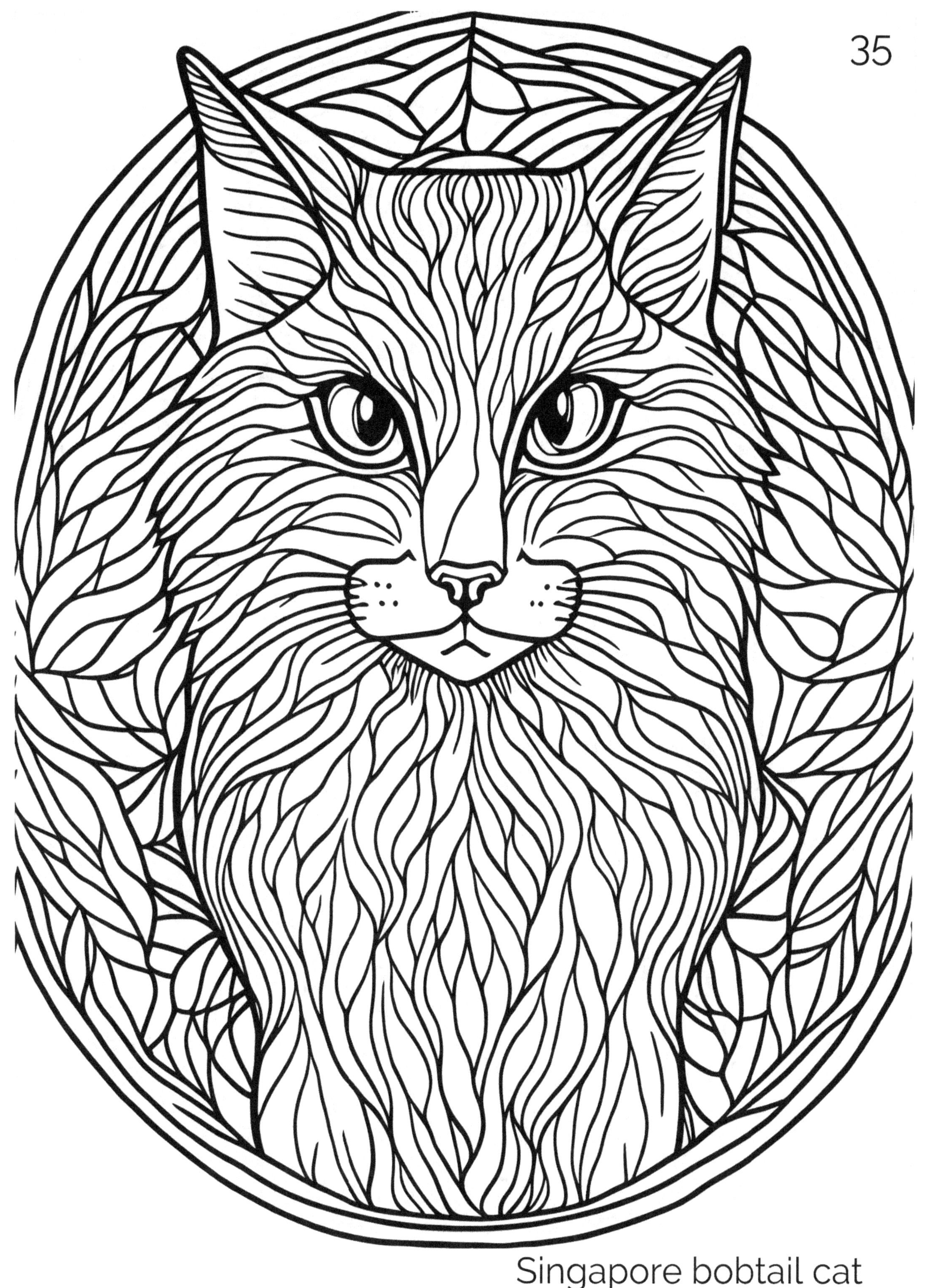

Singapore bobtail cat

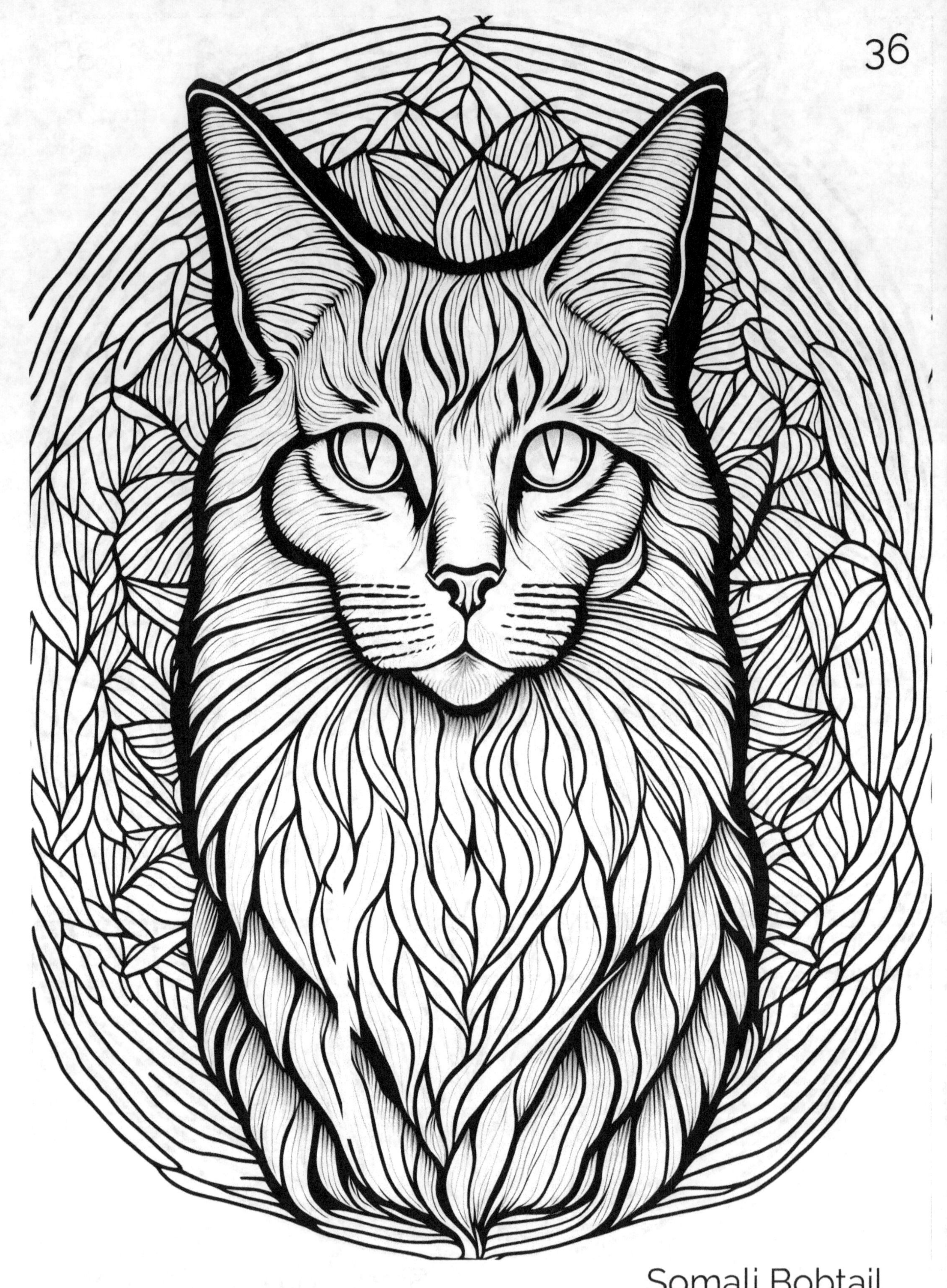

Somali Bobtail

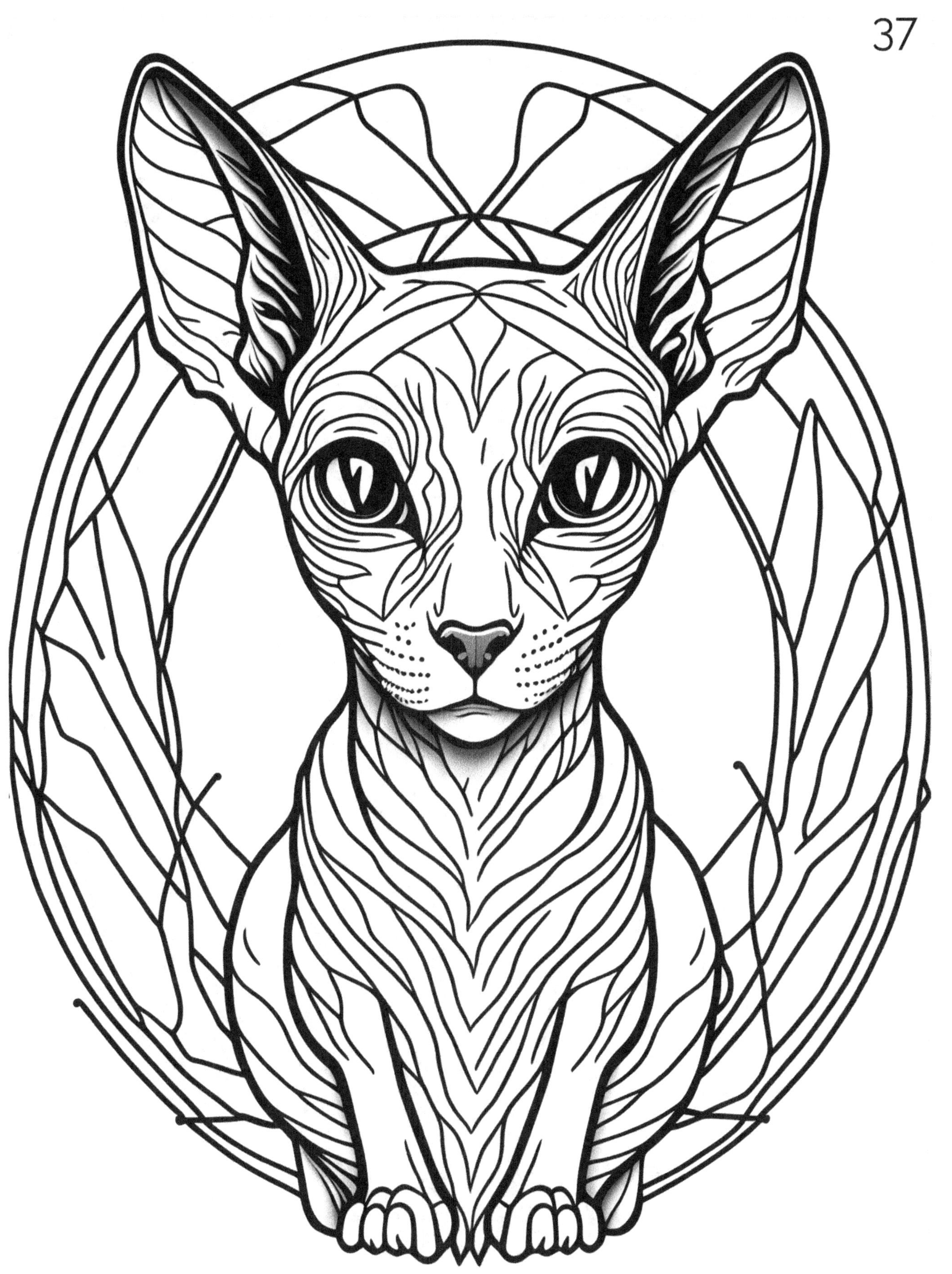

Sphynx bobtail cat

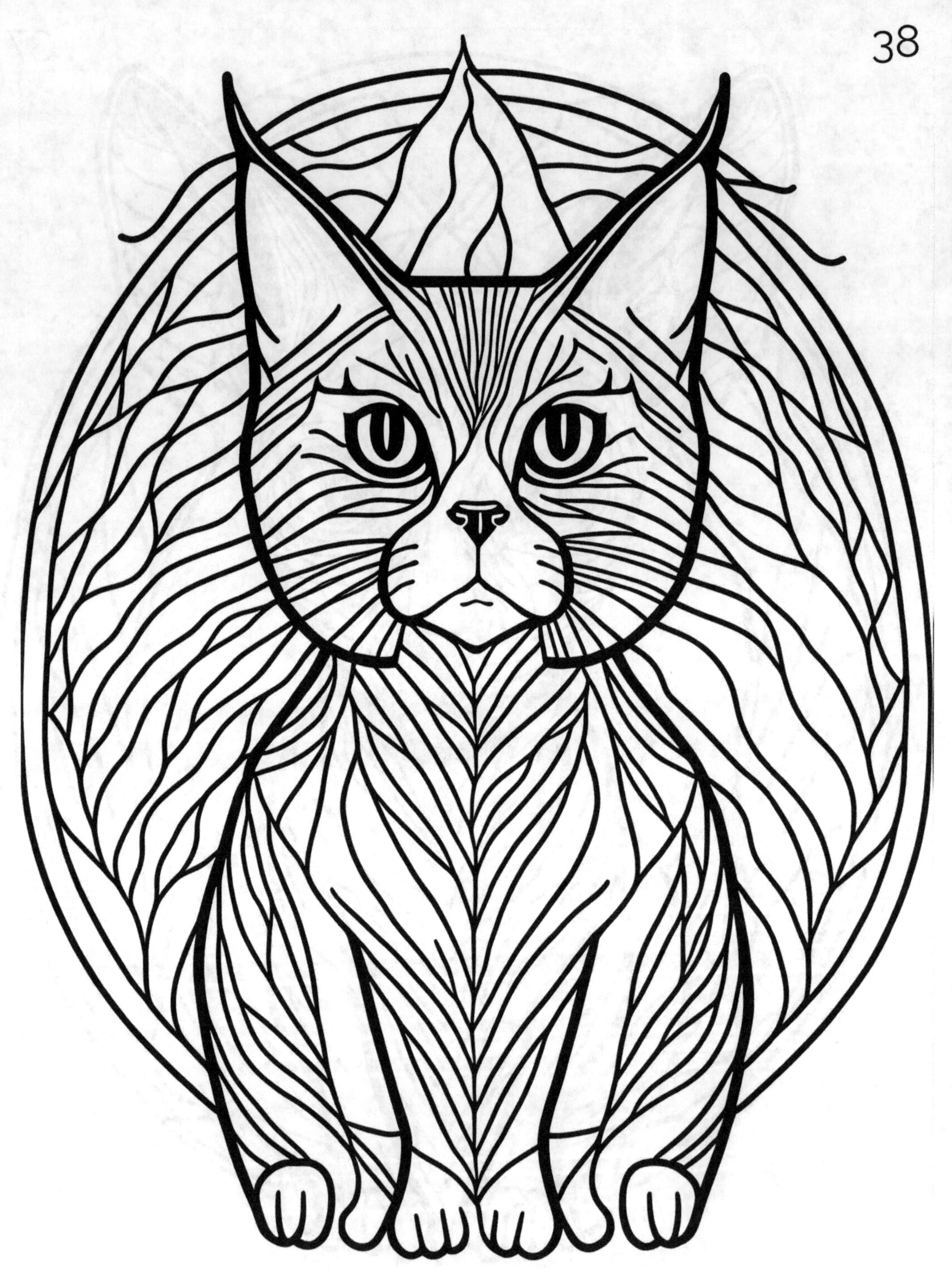

Turkish bobtail

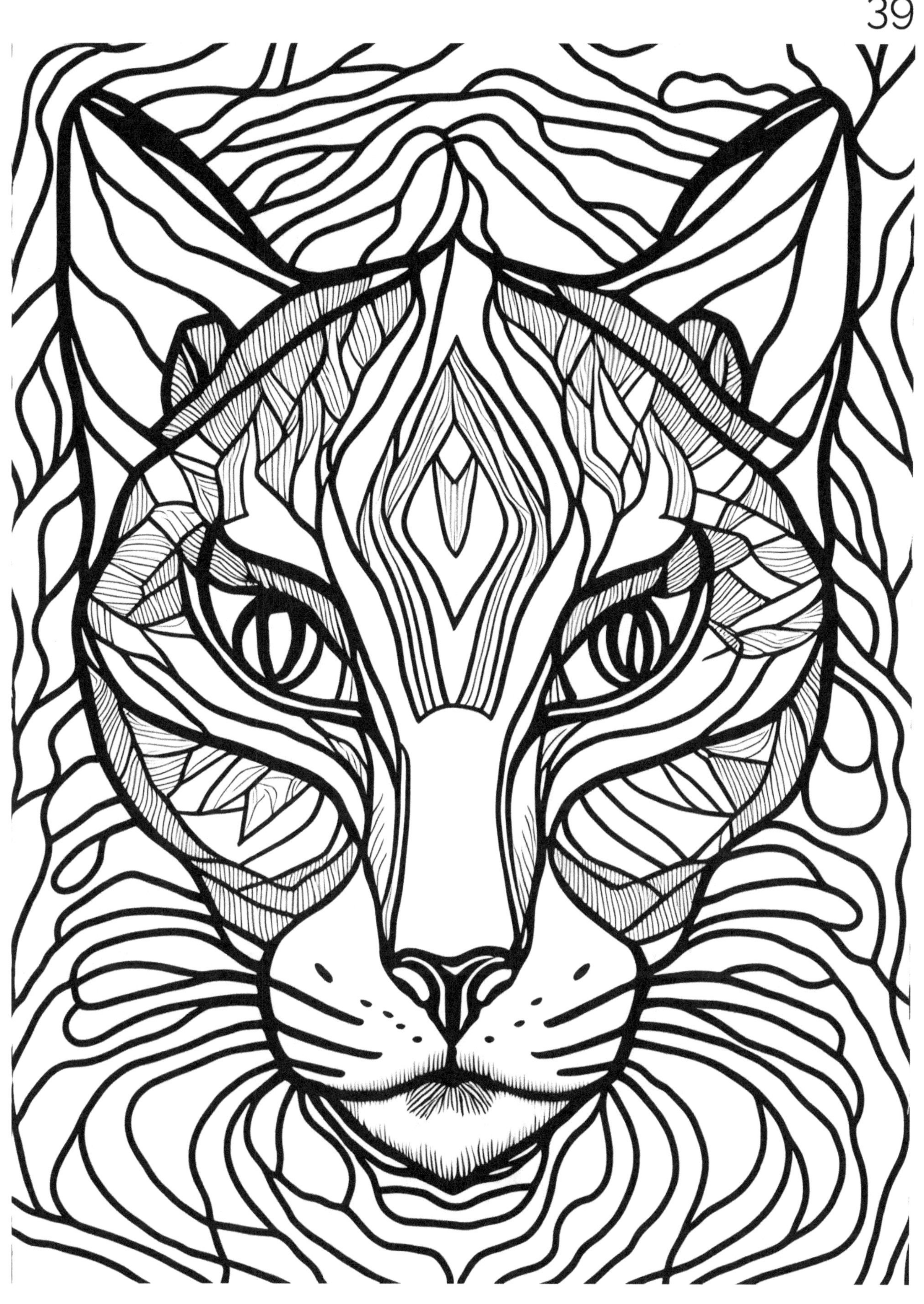

Wild cat

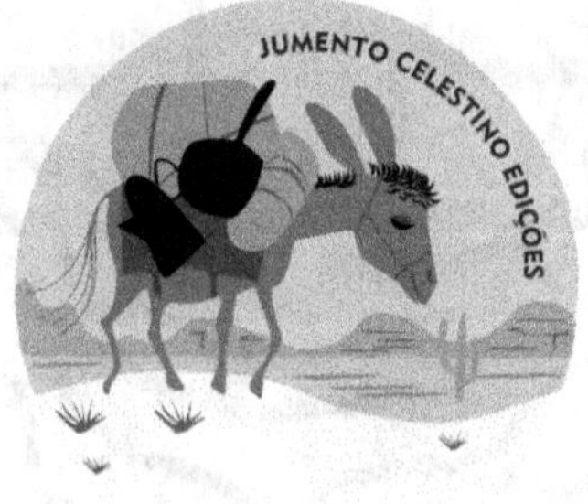

JUMENTO CELESTINO EDIÇÕES